IMAGES OF LEADERSHIP AND AUTHORITY FOR THE CHURCH

Biblical Principles and Secular Models

David A. Steele

UNIVERSITY
PRESS OF
AMERICA

LANHAM • NEW YORK • LONDON

Copyright © 1986 by

University Press of America,® Inc.

4720 Boston Way
Lanham, MD 20706

3 Henrietta Street
London WC2E 8LU England

Library of Congress Cataloging in Publication Data

Steele, David A., 1946-
  Images of leadership and authority for the church.

  Bibliography: p.
  Includes index.
  1. Church polity.   2. Authority (Religion)
3. Christian leadership.   4. Clergy—Office.   5. Laity.
I. Title.
BV650.2.S74   1986   262.1   86-24589
ISBN 0-8191-5710-4 (alk. paper)
ISBN 0-8191-5711-2 (pbk. : alk. paper)

All University Press of America books are produced on acid-free
paper which exceeds the minimum standards set by the National
Historical Publications and Records Commission.

This book is dedicated to the people of Pilgrim Congregational Church of Cambridge, Massachusetts, who contributed greatly to my growth as a pastor.

ACKNOWLEDGEMENTS

I am indebted to my wife, Barbara, for assistance in editing and patience with an overextended husband. I am also indebted to Dr. Meredith Handspiker for perceptive questions and critique. Other members of the faculty of Andover Newton Theological School have also influenced, through various classes and private consultations, both my conception of, and my functioning as, a pastor. Most particularly they have helped me to sort through my experiences and to crystallize my thinking as I searched for a handle on my concerns over authority in the church.

Finally, I wish to acknowledge that all references to the Bible have been taken from the Revised Standard Version, copyrighted 1946, 1952.

TABLE OF CONTENTS

PREFACE

This book examines a role definition for church
leadership and the nature of the authority which
accompanies that role. Particularly I am interested
in the shape which this role and authority needs to
take in order to satisfy the needs and expectations of
both pastor and congregation during the final years of
the twentieth century. My interest in this subject
has grown very much out of personal concerns with my
own functioning as a pastor. These concerns have
arisen largely due to the rubbing together of various
aspects of my own experience: an evangelical background and seminary training contrasted with the much
more liberal United Church of Christ in which I have
served; a social conscience developed during the midst
of university unrest contrasted with a small conserva-
tive urban congregation where I began as a pastor; an
interest in the lay renewal movement and its emphasis
on utilizing the gifts of the laity, contrasted with
Clinical Pastoral Education and its emphasis on pastoral office and authority. All these experiences
have left their imprint on me. They have both sur-
faced my concern and influenced the specific outcome
of my study.

David A. Steele

INTRODUCTION

Church leadership is currently in a stage of transition. Too little clarity exists, even regarding discernment of the right questions. Primarily this stems from differing perspectives on the professional ministry. Yet it also involves the relationship between these professionals and the lay leadership. This book will explore this confusion and suggest some contemporary images which may help inform those, both professional and lay, who would lead the church during the closing years of the twentieth century.

Professional pastoral ministry suffers today from the loss of a sense of accomplishment amidst an ever-increasing burden of busyness and pressure. There are many more involvements for the modern pastor than merely the preaching and pastoral calling of a simpler day. Yet despite the swamped feelings of many clergy there is still a high degree of unmet expectation. At times there is a lack of concrete results. Even when one can point to such fruits of one's labor, often there is no confirming consensus on the part of the congregation. Furthermore, the pastor is not always satisfied with the discernible consequences of his or her effort. The only accomplishments seem insignificant and meaningless when compared with what one set out to do. Thus it is inevitable that those in the pastorate today frequently struggle with confusion and frustration, hurt and anger; they are sometimes plagued with despondency and despair. Not only does this influence the clergy, but it has ramifications for the whole church and the effectiveness of its ministry.

It is of little surprise that an unprecedented number of clergy have recently decided to leave the profession. Their departure has prompted much recent concern over its future. Many of their former colleagues see this exodus as merely a symptom of the larger problem still confronting those within the pastoral ministry. One result of this concern has been an attempt to gain the insights of those who have left the pastorate in the hope that their contribution will help clarify the needs and problems of the clergy. The most notable of such studies is by Gerald Jud, Edgar Mills and Genevieve Burch entitled, Ex-pastors: Why Men Leave the Parish Ministry. For some of these ex-pastors, the reasons for leaving were personal ones, such as illness or divorce. But approximately half of the reasons given related directly to professional problems. Included among these problems were: a sense of personal and professional inadequacy, lack of an opportunity to put training and skills to fullest use, dissatisfaction of parish work, and a sense of being stultified by the church's lack of spiritual growth and relevance.[1] Lest we think that these difficulties are only the malady of dissidents, the authors are quick to assert that there was not much difference between pastors and ex-pastors in attitudes, beliefs, job dissatisfaction, role enjoyment, and search behavior. The only difference is that they live on the opposite sides of what the writers call "tipping point experiences."[2] These experiences are ones which produce an amount of frustration beyond which one has no hope within the pastoral ministry. All clergy have a tendency to fall prone to these experiences since they constantly live with a delicate balance between hope and disillusionment. This balancing process is inevitable in an occupation where one's entrance is always accompanied by great hopes and one's actual experience is accompanied by equally great frustration.

The ex-pastors studied by Jud, Mills and Burch placed equal responsibility on both the church and themselves for the failure.[3] Certainly responsibility does need to be shouldered by those involved in any endeavor. However, the causes for this sense of inadequacy go much deeper. There have been tremendous changes recently in the church as a whole, resulting from the influx of new secular approaches and methodologies, as well as from our changing understandings of faith. The speed with which the death of God theology came and went is but one recent illustration of the state of flux of modern theology and belief. Yet the turmoil within the church is merely a part of the general instability of institutions and values throughout our society.

Shifting values, with their concomitant influence upon family, church, and other institutions, could put a great deal of strain upon anyone. But stress is particularly acute upon those who spell out, maintain, and convey the values, primarily the clergy. The faith crisis shows itself in his or her own vacillating beliefs. The changing nature of family, church, and other structures of authority in our society has had its effects on the ability of the pastor to understand and accept the authority that comes with the calling. The changing relationships between the various professions, and how our society perceives the pastorate, has had its influence on the degree of respect the prospective clergyperson has for the integrity of the pastoral profession. These same changing interprofessional relationships, when coupled with the instability of the church and an oscillation of beliefs, leave one hard pressed to discern anything but a cloudy conception of the pastoral role.

It is not uncommon to hear and see clergy who do not know who they are or what they really believe. Some desire to abdicate their authority and be "the same as everyone else." Some prefer to see themselves primarily as counselors or social activists because they have lost any sense of integrity within the pastoral profession. Some are unsure of their own area of knowledge and skill and therefore try to solve all problems.

The frequent result is a person dictated to, and swayed by, superiors, peers, or laity. The pastor is often unable to resist the pressure to do the many biddings of diverse people. Much of the time these well-meaning Christian people do not agree. Thus the pastor is confronted with the impossibility of fulfilling a multitude of conflicting expectations. Some lay people involved in the lay renewal movement call for a redefinition of clergy and laity roles. Other lay people insist on the traditional lines of distinction. Seminary faculties are often divided between those emphasizing the priestly and prophetic roles. The Church is finding among its ranks those who no longer regard the preacher as the central image. Competing emphases include leading of small groups, social action, and pastoral care. Some church officials, when confronted with a small struggling church, would encourage meeting the needs of new people in the community in order to reverse decline. Others would see merger as the only solution for maintaining a meaningful ministry to those who have supported the church throughout their lifetimes. Still others would have the church close down to make room for a new structure more appropriate for today's needs. The words of Mark A. May, quoted by H. Richard Niebuhr some three decades ago, still ring true, "Entering the ministry is . . . like entering the army, where one never knows where he will land or live or what specific work he will be called to perform."[4]

To function effectively as a pastor these crises of faith, identity, professional integrity, role and authority need to be faced. Coming to terms with them involves much more than the attainment of a body of information. It necessitates the ability to practice from out of one's set of firm beliefs. It means being able to perceive where and how one fits into the ministry with his or her special identity. It involves appreciating the possibilities and limitations of the profession by accepting its integrity. It requires one to develop the necessary knowledge and skills to perform the role, learning to base one's success on a realistic and solid role conception. Finally, it necessitates an ability to personally accept the authority that comes with the role. In other words, personal appropriation is the final key.

All of these crises must become intensely personal at some point. However, two of them, identity and professional integrity, are fundamentally personal at heart. One's identity is not something to be researched in textbooks or spelled out in general terms that apply to everyone alike. Though there are some things to be said about the search for identity, it is important to leave this quest for one's own special character to the individual himself or herself. However, at some points it is helpful to indicate where one's own identity may become a factor in ascertaining one's own particular role. Secondly, this book is not intended to be a defense of the profession. The integrity of the pastoral calling, amply spelled out in James D. Glasse's book, Profession: Minister,[5] is simply an assumption from which I write. Yet some of the material of this book may be of help to those who would see the Biblical and historical material as validating their professional integrity.

The other three areas are not primarily personal. Instead they are issues over which one might well disagree with the people in one's congregation. In fact one's beliefs, authority, and role are never formed in isolation. There is always an interplay with the congregation which helps produce any finalized conceptions. Furthermore, any great differences in viewpoint concerning these matters will most certainly lead to a large degree of dissatisfaction on the part of both pastor and congregation. Thus it is especially important that all church leaders examine these areas objectively, as well as subjectively. However, compiling the kind of systematic theology needed to adequately address the faith question would require too much space for this book. Furthermore, one could easily differ on some theological tenets, yet still function effectively as a leader of the church.

Therefore, two concerns will be the focus of this book -- role and authority. The examination of authority will focus on three questions. The first question is: who grants the authority, what is its source? Ultimately it is God who bestows authority and power. Yet God does this through human means which, themselves, then become more tangible, penultimate sources. The three traditional sources of authority are the church, the Scriptures, or an individual person. All of these are always in existence to some degree. The question is to ask which one is, or should be, predominant. The second question is: to whom is the authority given, who is the recipient? This raises the issue of distinction between clergy and laity and the exact nature of the authority given to each. The third question investigates the basis of authority. Again there are two traditional answers: the charismatic authority based on gift or ability, and the official authority based on place or office. Here it will be important to look at the interrelationship of these two and ask what is the best basis today.

The search for a contemporary conception of the role of church leadership must begin with an examination of ministry as a whole. One cannot begin to talk about the specifics of a particular role within the ministry of the church until that is accomplished. Then, as in looking at any role, one must set out the various component parts or functions. Yet one must not stop there. As H. Richard Neibuhr has pointed out, whenever the pastorate has functioned effectively, one of the functions has been perceived as central. The others have been ordered, not around it, but around that purpose which the central function served.[6] Therefore, it will be important in this study to discuss the basic societal needs of various periods of history as well as those of our own time. First, one must establish the connection between basic needs and predominant pastoral functions in the past. Second, one needs to suggest a predominant, focal function for the pastoral role today, the one around which, and toward which, everything else should build. Finally it is important to see exactly how the other functions fit in and how the whole role model can be adapted to the needs, gifts, abilities, and character of particular churches and individuals.

In order to gain a proper understanding of both role and authority, one needs to ascertain the essential character of the pastoral calling. To better understand this, one needs to look extensively at the normative beginnings of this calling as recorded in the Christian Scriptures, and the development of the profession down through church history. By clarifying the Biblical principles and historical influences, one can begin to understand the roots from which today's model must emerge. Another requirement for a proper understanding is an adequate knowledge of contemporary needs and some conceptions as to how they might be met. One can gain insight into the nature of these needs, and how to meet them, by looking once more to the past history of the church. In addition to this, it can be helpful to look at some contemporary secular professions which attempt to meet similar needs. While doing this one must take care to preserve the uniqueness of the pastoral calling. Yet, if one can avoid the temptation to create mirror images of other roles, there is much to be learned.

Thus the outline of this book can be clearly seen. Part I will trace the historical development of leadership role and authority beginning with the Biblical norms. Part II, building on this foundation, will initially propose an ideal contemporary conception of the same. An examination of contemporary needs, as well as some secular occupations and how they meet those needs, will be used to enrich our understanding of both role and authority. The last chapter will then draw together the various insights and speak to the question of how we can arrive at a final formulation.

1. Gerald J. Jud, Edgar W. Mills, Jr. and Genevieve Walters Burch, <u>Ex-pastors: Why Men Leave the
Parish Ministry</u> (Philadelphia: United Church Press,
1970), pp. 50-51.

2. <u>Ibid</u>., p. 107.

3. <u>Ibid</u>., p. 51.

4. H. Richard Niebuhr, <u>The Purpose of the Church
and Its Ministry: Reflections on the Aims of Theological Education</u> (New York: Harper & Brothers, 1956),
p. 51.

5. James D. Glasse, <u>Profession: Minister</u> (Nashville and New York: Abingdon Press, 1968).

6. Niebuhr, pp. 58-59.

PART I

HISTORICAL DEVELOPMENT

CHAPTER I

ROLE AND AUTHORITY IN THE NEW TESTAMENT

The development of leadership roles and authority in the New Testament is a process. No one conception exists throughout the record. Therefore it is important to show the various stages of that development. Within each stage, one must delineate the function of church leaders, as well as address the issues of authority. First, though, an understanding of the conception of ministry itself must be the starting point of any investigation of role or authority.

Understanding of Ministry

Choice of Terms Denoting Ministry

The usual Greek terms denoting officialdom are conspicuously missing in the New Testament record: ἀρχή, used to imply a primacy in rank; τιμή, used to describe the honor and dignity of office; and τέλος, used to mean the total power of office. Even the word for minister, λειτουργός, is used only once to refer to an office holder in the church. Instead the New Testament writers chose a secular word, "service" (διάκονος), with which to speak of ministry. This term, unlike the others, does not describe an elite group, for it carries no overtones of rule of officialdom. It is used to describe the role of servant who dutifully waits on one's master at the table. Such a picture would startle the mind of a first century person even more than it does ours. For the distinction is great between a Greek master and slave of that time. The master lays on the bed, while the servant brings the food. From this, one can conclude that New Testament office holders are primarily fellow believers rather than dignitaries. Any official rank is second in importance, at best, and connotes service, rather than domination, of the church. This servanthood affects not only the manner in which a leader functions, but also the actual choice of responsibilities with which one is entrusted. Priestly or cultic functions are no longer part of the responsibilities of leadership; the terms denoting this function are conspicuously absent.[1]

3

New Concept of Priesthood

Διάκονος, by its very tone implies a position of service to one another on the part of all. Ministry is expected on the part of all Christians throughout the New Testament. The priesthood of all believers is emphasized in 1 Pet. 2:5-9. "You are the light of the world" (Mt. 5:14) is spoken to all followers of Jesus. Sole access to God through certain ritual ceremonies is no longer the right of one select group, as in Judaism, " . . . for through him (Christ) we both (Jews and Gentiles) have access in one Spirit to the Father." (Eph. 2:18). Each one can be instructed directly by the Lord (1 Jn. 2:27), empowered to speak the word of God oneself (Acts 4:31, 8:4, 11:19, and Mt. 10:27) and teach others in the community (Heb. 5:12). Each person is expected to take part in the worship services by choosing hymns and giving a lesson or testimony (1 Cor. 14:26). "Go and baptize" is a command given to all disciples (Mt. 28:19). So Philip, an evangelist, but not one of the elders, baptizes the Ethiopian eunuch (Acts 8). "Do this in remembrance of me" (Lk. 22:19), is a call to the whole church to celebrate the Lord's Supper. Thus, the entire Corinthian church, not just its leaders, receives directions concerning the observance of the Lord's Supper (1 Cor. 11). The priestly task of mediating between humankind and God is now the responsibility of all Christians in Christ (Hebrews). The charge of forgiving sins (Mt. 18:18) is given as a directive to the whole church. Prayer is expected on the part of all Christians for others both within and outside the community (Acts 2:42 and 1 Tim. 2:1). Every believer is required to make those sacrifices which the Old Testament regarded as priestly in nature: praise, thanksgiving, prayer, justice, kindness, and love (Heb. 13:15, 2 Tim. 4:6, 1 Thess. 5:17-18, and Rev. 8:3). As a Christian, one's whole life must be offered as "a living sacrifice, holy, and acceptable to God, which is your spiritual worship." (Rom. 12:1).

Uncertainty over the need for a person or group of people to act as leader(s) may follow from this definition of ministry. Yet the New Testament does clearly present us with the existence of such people. While a ruling class with absolute authority never exists, persons who function in a leadership capacity are present at all stages of the development of the early church.

4

Church Leadership in Palestine

The authority of church leaders in Palestine, as in all of the early church, began with the person of Jesus. Jesus's own authority was not at all official. He did not hold a universally recognized position and did not appeal to any official commissioning. Though he laid claim to being the Lord, the Son of Man, the Son of God, the long awaited Messiah, these were not clearly delineated offices in the minds of the Jewish people. Instead, his actions formed the primary basis for his authority. Therefore, his authority was fundamentally charismatic in nature.

Leadership Titles

During Jesus's ministry he personally called and commissioned twelve men to be his apostles (ἀπόστολοι). Later others, such as Matthias (Acts 1), who were eye-witnesses of Jesus' earthly ministry, became part of this core group.[2] These apostles were the first leaders of the church. However, they did not inherit apostleship on the basis of gifts or abilities. Nor was this any officially recognized position. The apostles created an organization, but they themselves were prior to it.[3] Thus, the basis of their authority lay neither in charisma nor office, but simply in the existence of the personal call from the Lord. Furthermore, the aim of apostolic authority is not subjection, but fellowship. Thus no rigid monarchical hierarchy emerged within the apostolate. Jesus did become closer to some than others, and Peter did take the role of spokesman in the very beginning of the church. But there were other apostles, such as John, who gained prominence as well. Plus James, the Lord's brother, shared great authority alongside Peter in Jerusalem, finally succeeding Peter in his capacity as head leader.[4] Hence, a plurality of leadership under a single head existed among the apostles. Each recognized the particular abilities or gifts of the others, especially those of Peter. Yet they shared overall leadership.

At a later point in time, elders (πρεσβύτεροι), apparently appeared first in the church in Jerusalem.[5] Exactly when they originated is indefinite. Possibly some Jewish elders became Christians (Acts 6:7) and came to see themselves, then, as true elders. At the very latest they existed at the time the collection was brought to Jerusalem in Acts 11. At this point in time, the Christian elders had patterned themselves after the elders in a synagogue who were in charge of administrative and disciplinary matters. Thus, the hellenistic Jews in Jerusalem were probably the ones responsible for introducing this office. Later, the model shifted to the Sanhedrin as the Jerusalem church increasingly judaised after the departure of Peter.[6] At the time of the New Testament, the elders in the Sanhedrin were the least influential group, after the priests and scribes. Thus "elders" became a special term for the lay members of that body, which was the highest court of authority in Judaism. The Sanhedrin did not have any official leader, yet the high priest did preside "ex-officio." In Acts 15 the Christian elders, under the direction of James, acted in this governing capacity toward the entire church at the Council of Jerusalem.[7] James was never referred to as a high priest, yet he was unmistakably the leader of leaders. Jewish custom, in fact, may have produced the expectation that James would take the place of his brother, Jesus.[8] Thus the Palestinian church developed very definite conceptions of office and authority. Although some have proposed that the book of Acts is historically inaccurate in referring to elders, they have still affirmed the Palestinian origins of Christian office.[9]

The Palestinian church also undoubtedly used some secondary names for its leaders. Philip is referred to as an evangelist (Acts 8 and 21:8). Agabus is called a prophet (Acts 11:27-30 and 21:10 ff.). The seven chosen in Acts 6 are given the ministry of service, διακονέω resembling somewhat the function elsewhere described by the title "deacon." The presence of these terms in the early Palestinian church could be due to editorializing by the historian, Luke. Yet it was still possible that they had some place in the primitive community in Jerusalem. Finally, the early Christian Church of Palestine probably knew of, and utilized, the shepherd (ποιμήν) imagery to describe its leaders. Certainly, they must have been familiar with Jesus' parable about the shepherd going out after the one sheep that was lost. They also may have known about Jesus' call to Peter to "feed my sheep." The term "shepherds" was used to refer to the rulers and leaders of the Hebrew people, including those of later Judaism.[10] It was not a title, but a description of the task of the leader and a very good portrayal of the developing office of elder in the Palestinian Church.

Source of Authority

Ordination was a second institution which the Church borrowed from Judaism. Both the elders[11] and scribes[12] in Judaism had students whom they later elected as their replacements and then ordained by the laying on of hands and intercessory prayer. This act of ordination was the mode by which they conferred authority and power. In the New Testament those who commissioned the seven in Acts 6:3-6, and appointed the elders to the Pauline churches, used this laying on of hands. Thus an individual person(s) became the primary giver of authority to, not only the apostles, but to the elders as well. The needs of the primitive church gave good reason to expect this primacy of an authority given by individuals. It was a time of much rapid change, thus creating a need for order and for quick, clear cut decisions.

Summary

The need for order in the early Palestinian church inevitably led to the creation of a leadership structure. This leadership consisted primarily of, first, apostles and, later, elders, with other titles being used less frequently. The basis of authority for the leadership became official rather than charismatic when the transition was made from apostles to elders. At first the developing structure emphasized the plurality of leadership. However, to facilitate decisiveness, the Palestinian church began to bestow special authority on an "ex-officio" head. Plurality of leadership was retained, but alongside it there developed the leader of leaders. This growing influence of the single leader was also reflected in their understanding that the source of authority lay with the individual.

Church Leadership in Paul's Epistles

Basis of Authority

The uncontested letters of Paul never mention elders. Yet Paul did refer to other leaders, giving them definite names. These names did not relate as much to office or title as they did to the function performed within the community. No traditional office automatically qualified its bearers to lead the church. Instead, God gave to each individual the gifts (χαρίσματα) necessary to fulfill a particular

7

ministry.[13]   However, a rating system did exist among the various charismata.   Paul gave apostles first priority, prophets second and teachers third in 1 Cor. 12:28.   The greater the service to others in the community, the higher Paul regarded the gift. Furthermore, no fixed and final listing of these charismata existed anywhere in Paul's writings.   In fact, the various lists (1 Cor. 12:28-31; Rom. 12:6-8; Eph. 4:11) differed a great deal.   Finally, the distinctions between the various charismata were not clearly delineated.   A prophet could at times teach and a teacher could prophesy.   Paul himself functioned in many capacities.

Paul probably used this system of charismatic authority in opposition to some other early Christian conception of church order.[14]   Yet the Pauline churches were not the only ones with this form of church government.   In fact, Paul could have taken over this charismatic approach from the church at Antioch where prophets and teachers, rather than elders, sent him out to minister to the gentiles (Acts 13:1-3).   The church in Rome, also not founded by Paul, was a second example of the widespread lack of a special order of office holders.   At least Paul's letter to the Romans, despite many personal greetings, never mentioned any such officials.

Paul's emphasis on freedom for his congregations put greater limits on the degree of authority he was willing to recognize.   Yet being an apostle was very important to him.   Therefore, at times, he did defend his authority, as well as that of others who worked with him.   However, he did so only by pointing to Christ, and not to an established order which had ordained him.   Furthermore, he was not ashamed to identify himself with non-apostles or to abandon any authority, even his own, whenever it ran the risk of undermining the gospel (Gal. 1:8-9).[15]   The bases of authority for Paul were one's call and one's ability to perform a particular ministry in the community, rather than one's status.   Even the basis of authority for an apostle was charismatic.   For, to Paul, an apostle was anyone who had seen the risen Lord and had been commissioned by Him,[16] rather than one who had the position, or status, of being with Jesus during his earthly ministry.

The letters to the church at Corinth provide an excellent example of Paul's charismatic authority and multiplicity of leadership.   No elders, bishops or

8

deacons are present. In these letters Paul never addressed a single leader or group of leaders, even when the subject matter concerned the creation or restoration of order. Instead, he spoke to all the Christians about such matters as administering the Lord's Supper (1 Cor. 11), preaching and speaking in tongues (1 Cor. 14), church discipline (1 Cor. 6:5, 2 Cor. 2:6), the delivering of alms (1 Cor. 16:3, 2 Cor. 8 and 9), and the settling of disputes within the community (1 Cor. 1-3). It appears each person was equally responsible for whatever happened. Paul would single out a particular individual only when that person was not properly exercising his or her special gift.

Source of Authority

God was the ultimate giver of authority from Paul's perspective, as from any proper Christian understanding. The gift was of the Spirit, not of the church, the apostle, or anyone else. Thus, the authority to exercise a gift was the right of any person who had a call from God and could demonstrate it by the ability to use the gift properly. As a result, a large group of diverse people often shared the leadership. The only control that the church had was its call to test the gifts and discern between the true and false manifestations of the Spirit. Thus the community itself became the predominant human bestower of authority. Comprised of Jews and gentiles, slave and free, rich and poor, the Pauline churches must have had a great need for community building. Consequently, they were fertile ground for the development of the community as the primary grantor of authority.

No set pattern apparently existed for determining who should take on various ministries. In some cases, the church chose persons, such as Titus's selection to be a fellow worker with Paul (2 Cor. 8:19). In other cases, the church approved the voluntary services of persons like Stephanas and his family (2 Cor. 16:15-16). Finally, even Paul gained his authority partly from the community, despite his insistence that his calling came from no human being. It was the church at Antioch which recognized the gift given to Paul and sent him out. Furthermore, Paul continually defended his apostleship in his dialogue with the various churches which he served, thus indicating his felt need for their approval.

Various Charismata

In addition to the apostles, Paul held the ministries of prophets (προφῆται) and teachers (διδάσκαλοι) in greatest esteem. Both of these were preachers of the Word, within the limits of the apostolic witness. The teacher's task was to hand on and interpret the tradition for the purpose of general instruction. The prophets were less limited than the teachers in their expression. Their function was to speak, on the basis of revelation, words of edification, encouragement, and consolation within a particular concrete situation (1 Cor. 14:3, 26-30). They proclaimed intuitively as opposed to the more systematic exposition of the teachers.[17]

Alongside these preaching ministries, Paul specified ministries of guidance and welfare. He referred in 1 Thess. 5:12 to "those who are over you," terminology used in secular Greek to mean those taking care of someone's welfare.[18] Elsewhere he spoke of "he who gives aid" (Rom. 12:8) and helpers and administrators, the art of steering or guiding (1 Cor. 12:28). This imprecise terminology did not imply a fixed office, as no form of commissioning appeared to exist. Yet it did give the impression of a permanent ministry of leadership which consistently cared for the community. Respect and esteem (1 Thess. 5:12) were called for toward those who ministered in this capacity.[19] In one such case the authority of these persons appeared to be based on, not only charisma, but also longevity. The Corinthians were instructed to be subject to the family of Stephanas, who were the first converts in Achaia and had devoted themselves to the service of the church people (1 Cor. 16:15-16). Originally, the congregation must have seen in them the gift of guiding the church. Later the respect given them due to length of service must have become a natural part of the basis of authority itself.

Beginning of Official Basis

Eventually, the early Pauline Church began to describe the people who cared for the church by using official sounding terms. In Rom. 16:1 Paul referred to Phoebe as a deaconess, and in Philippians 1:1 he addressed his letter to the overseers, or bishops, (ἐπίσκοποι) and deacons (διάκονοι), as well as to the other saints. These overseers and deacons appeared to correspond to the administrators and helpers of earlier Pauline letters.[20] At least the tasks of these persons were administering and giving aid respectively. Evidently, by the time of this later letter to the Philippians, the degree of respect for "those over you" had grown beyond the level suggested by Paul's reference to Stephanas. The overseers and deacons at Philippi probably had had these gifts for a long time. Consequently, Paul could refer to them by the activities they did, as well as by the resulting esteem they acquired.[21] They had now come to be unquestionably characterized by the designation. Otherwise Paul had no purpose for tacking onto the greeting two words commonly used by the Greeks as titles.[22]

Yet these terms were probably still very imprecise and indefinite. Paul never addressed them with specific charges or responsibilities. Neither did he assume that they had jurisdiction over certain matters, such as the collection for the Jerusalem Church. (Phil. 2:25 and 4:18). The validity, and thus the authority, of these ministries still rested on the fact that God had given them by the Spirit. Even when a gift had become a continuing feature of church life, the authority that came with it could not be handed on.[23]

Summary

Paul's focus on the gifts of the Spirit fundamentally influenced his understanding of church leadership. The roles were many and various, though centering primarily around gifts of teaching, prophecy administration and helping. The resulting charismatic basis of authority did undergo some change as time passed. In his later epistles Paul used some official sounding terms. Yet the title bearers were never charged with specific responsibilities and the terms used in the designation were quite imprecise. Throughout the Pauline literature the recipients of authority were always listed in the plural and the source of authority continued to be the community which tested and recognized gifts.

Interlocking of the Two Traditions

In Acts

One of the earliest stages in the interlocking of the Palestinian and Pauline traditions is recorded in Acts 20:17-28. Here, the leaders in Ephesus were

11

called elders (vs. 17) and then told to feed (ποιμαίνειν) the flock, "in which the Holy Spirit has made you guardians (ἐπίσκοποι)" (vs. 28). The exact stage of development at the time of Paul's visit to the Ephesians was confused by the fact that Luke wrote the account a while after the event. Despite the fact that Luke includes himself in Paul's company in this section of the book, Luke is known for his editorializing in other sections. Undoubtedly, it was Luke's concern to join together the two traditions for the sake of church unity and the combatting of heresy.[24] Possibly he saw the origins of the later title bearers in these leaders at Ephesus, and therefore felt free to use the terms in describing them.

Paul himself must have spoken to a definite circle of leaders, outlining their tasks and responsibilities.[25] He quite likely used terms that included the responsibilities of the later elders and overseers. Possibly he could have used the term overseer, as he did in Phil. 1:1, or even the term elder in a patriarchal sense. This word, πρεσβύτερος, also meant "old Man". Thus Paul could easily have used this term to describe someone with longevity of service such as Stephanas. This patriarchal form of office, with its authority based on longevity, was the first stage of such development within the Pauline churches.[26]

In Hebrews and Ephesians

Pauline tradition, if not authorship, continued in the epistles to the Hebrews and Ephesians. Hebrews reflected the Pauline perspective by using the very general term, leaders (ἡγούμενοι), to describe the local authorities (13:7). The author requested submission to these leaders who were responsible for watching over the people (vs. 17). Certain signs, though, indicated that things were changing. The writer needed to inform all the people that they were expected to take part in the ministry of teaching (5:12). He even needed to tell them to go to worship (10:25). Furthermore, a fixed liturgical form was already in practice, and there were warnings of false doctrine and cases of apostasy.[27]

Ephesians provides us with a good picture of this transition in a Pauline church. A listing of church leaders in 4:11-12 included apostles, prophets, evangelists (εὐαγγελισταί), pastors (ποιμένες) and teachers. All of these were now clearly recognized

12

functions. The author still referred to these ministries as gifts of the Spirit in the usual Pauline
fashion. Yet the function of them all was to "equip
the believers for the work of ministry, for building
up the body of Christ." Clearly the functions of all
these, though still distinct enough to warrant separate names, had begun to blend together. Furthermore,
the writer included the word "some" (τοὺς δε) prior to
each of the names, with the exception of "teachers,"
thus giving "pastors" and "teachers" a common article.
By doing this, the author implied that these two terms
referred to the same persons.[28] This is especially
interesting when one notes the presumed connection, at
that time, between pastor (ποιμήν) and bishop/overseer
(ἐπίσκοπος).[29] Thus, for the first time, the early
church may have linked teaching, one of Paul's primary
ministries, to the administrative function of overseeing.

In 1 Peter, 2 Peter and Jude

The Catholic epistles show us a further development of this process in both Asia Minor, Paul's
mission field, and the eastern church. 1 Peter 5:1-5,
written to Asia Minor, finds the same three terms
interlocked that appeared in Acts 20:17 and 28. Here
the elders received the task of "tending (ποιμάνατε)
the flock of God that is your charge (ἐπισκοποῦντες)."
However, more organization existed here than in Acts
20. Gifts were still mentioned (4:10), but were
limited to preaching and practical service (4:9). The
elders had definitely developed into a patriarchal
form of office, as seen by the injunction to the
"younger" to be subject to the elders (5:5). Furthermore, these elders had disciplinary powers (5:3) and a
status equivalent to the author himself (5:1). Thus,
they had, by this time, assumed an authority comparable only to that of the apostles.

In a later development the elders appeared to
entirely replace the apostles, and therefore became
the sole chief authorities (2 Pet. 3:2, Jude 17).
Yet they based their message on the apostolic tradition for which they had become the guardians, a point
of view also depicted in the pastoral epistles (2
Tim. 2:2 and 4:6). Thus the tradition, which eventually became the Scripture, was now the primary
source of authority. The community still played a
role by deciding what or who represented tradition,
but it no longer seemed to be predominant. This
change can be understood in the light of the growing

13

need for stability and rootedness. This was a time of emerging heresies, external persecution and growing distance between the church and its origins. Hence tradition naturally became the predominant source of authority.

In 2 John and 3 John

The second and third epistles of John are especially informative as they represent an author, who was an elder somewhere in Asia Minor, writing to a church located more to the east. The author reflects the western development of the patriarchal elder who assumed special authority and dignity on the basis of age and longevity. Yet he was still the charismatic person, functioning much as a prophet or teacher. Like the prophets and teachers, who were diminishing in number, this author exercised his authority beyond merely his own local congregation.

In the eastern church, to whom the letters were addressed, we find a more powerful authority figure in the person of Diotrephes (3 John 9). Although the author attempted to override him, probably on the basis of his charismatic conception of authority, Diotrephes was obviously a powerful official with the right to excommunicate people (vs. 10). His conception of authority did not seem to extend beyond his own congregation.[30] Yet he, along with Titus and Timothy in the pastoral epistles, was the closest figure in the New Testament to the monarchical bishop of later times.[31]

In James and the Gospel of Matthew

The epistle of James and the Gospel of Matthew further reflect the development in the eastern church. James spoke of definite officials: teachers in 3:1 and elders in 5:14. Yet they had a charismatic quality about them. The teachers, if they were a continuation of those mentioned in Acts 13, were charismatic in origin. The elders, on the other hand, possessed the charismatic gift of healing as a result of their office (5:14).

Matthew gives us a picture of powerful authority on the part of the church leaders of this same period (16:18-19 and 18:15-18). The references to the church in these passages must represent the influence of the later time period during which Matthew wrote. In 16:18-19 Matthew portrays Jesus as placing Peter in

14

charge of the church. Jesus would build his church on this potentially promising apostle to whom he was giving the Keys to the Kingdom and the authority to forgive sins. In 18:15-18 Matthew's Jesus places church discipline in the hands of the same disciples who can bind or loose sins. In conclusion, the eastern church, like the western, developed a strong conception of office. Yet, it did not totally dismiss the charismatic influence.

In the Pastoral Epistles

The fullest expression of the final stage of leadership development in the New Testament is in the pastoral epistles. In these letters the name, "overseer," re-emerged as a designation for part, if not all, of the elders. Similarly, the author of the letter to Titus substituted the term "overseer" (bishop) for the term "elders" (1:5&7). The only problem in completely equating them is that "overseer" is singular and "elders" is plural. Possibly, the overseer was the leader of the elders, yet still one of them himself.[32] The author of 1 Timothy supports this theory when he writes, "Let the elders who rule well be considered worthy of double honor." (5:17). This double honor could have been the awarding of the position of overseer to those elders who ruled, as opposed to those who did not. If this were so, then the Pauline churches, at this time, had a very similar kind of leadership to the early church in Jerusalem under James. Both probably gave overall leadership to a number of people, yet specified one person as "leader of leaders."

Having determined that all overseers were elders, we can conclude that both eldership and overseeing were a part of the developing function of both the bishop/pastor and a small group of leader colleagues. The church certainly perceived any tasks assumed by these named officials as pastoral in nature. The most common function named by this author was teaching (1 Tim. 3:2, 5:17 and Tit. 1:9), though he also referred to it as a charismatic gift based on ability (2 Tim. 2:2). Others which he listed included the care of the church (1 Tim. 3:5), practical and economic affairs (Tit. 1:7), preaching (or prophecy) and the ability to rule (1 Tim. 5:17). Though the New Testament never refers to Titus or Timothy as bishops, their rule and authority closely resembled these pastoral leaders. They were responsible for church discipline and teaching (2 Tim. 2:2, 25; Tit. 2:1-15).

Yet unlike bishops, they did not seem limited to one community (1 Tim. 1:3, Tit. 1:5). Hence, it is reasonably safe to add tasks given to them to the list of pastoral responsibilities. These functions included: evangelism (2 Tim. 4:5), the public reading of Scripture (1 Tim. 4:13), plus the appointment, ordination and oversight of elders (1 Tim. 5:17-22, Tit. 1:5).

By the time of these epistles, an official basis of authority, resembling that of the Jewish office of elder, found its way into the very churches begun by Paul. The author of 1 Timothy actually referred to "overseer" as an office (3:1). In most cases this office had even lost its former patriarchal character. The author did occasionally use the term "elder" in the sense of "old man" (1 Tim. 5:1) and admonished Timothy to respect such persons. However, for the first time, a young man like Timothy (1 Tim. 4:12) could aspire to a position such as overseer (1 Tim. 3:1). Furthermore, the conception of office had become precise enough for the author of these epistles to distinguish between at least two separate offices, overseer and deacon. This rather rapid development of official authority happened, in part, because the church needed an authority based on something other than subjective experience in order to provide a defense against ungodly spontaneity. Consequently they entrusted the ministries of ordering the community into the hands of dependable people through the use of an ordination rite. This laying on of hands, taken over from the Palestinian church, signified the imparting of the Spirit's power to help the recipient administer that which had been entrusted.[33]

Although the basis of authority had become increasingly official, two factors still stood in the way of this office becoming too sacred. First, the church did not lose the concept of charisma, but fused it with the official basis of authority. Timothy's mentor warned him not to neglect the gift given to him at his ordination (1 Tim. 4:14), and then told him to rekindle it (2 Tim. 1:6). Although a certain degree of authority was given him on the basis of pure office, another part would only be recognized as he demonstrated his ability. Second, these officials could not become overly authoritative because they did not legitimate themselves. The tradition of sound apostolic doctrine (Tit. 1:9, 2 Tim. 1:13), the basis for our present Scripture, was their primary source of authority.[34]

Summary

The interlocking of the Palestinian and Pauline traditions began gradually with the imprecise use of official terminology in the former Pauline churches and the addition of charismatic gifts to the functioning of elders in the eastern church. By the end of the New Testament period both eastern and western churches had adopted a balance of official and charismatic bases of authority. Due to the need for rootedness and stability, the source of this authority increasingly came from the tradition, which was to become Scripture. Furthermore, while the whole church maintained the plurality of leadership, it also universally adopted the "ex-officio" leader of leaders. Finally, the functioning of all these leaders began to center around tasks which represented a combination of both former traditions.

Normative Conclusions for Post-biblical Times

The pastoral epistles give us the fullest expression of the union of the two basic strands of tradition. It is prior to the point when some functions, as well as a charismatic understanding of authority, nearly passed into disuse. It is the optimum point in the interlocking process and the final stage of development included in the scriptural canon. Consequently, these pastoral epistles are the best model for any later conceptions of leadership role and authority.

Authority of Church Leadership

As mentioned above, the pastoral epistles provide us with a good balance between the charismatic and official, but non-patriarchal, conceptions of the basis of authority. The church needs the official aspect of authority to keep in line the charismatic tendency toward unchecked spontaneity, a lesson learned by the early Pauline churches. It needs the charismatic authority to keep the office holder continually responsible for the way in which one exercises one's gifts, a lesson learned by the Palestinian church. A disproportionate emphasis on either of these elements, at the expense of the other, leads to difficulties. An overemphasis either way will undermine the ultimate basis of authority, Christ himself. [35]

17

The pastoral epistles retain the plurality of leadership, common to the whole New Testament, and crucial to a correct understanding of ministry through the priesthood of all believers. Yet, the single leadership of one person, modeled after James in Jerusalem, begins to take shape in these originally Pauline churches. Hence, this model not only preserves the multiplicity of input and insight into the leadership of the church, but also provides a vehicle for quick, clear, and decisive action through a single, primary, yet non-dictatorial, authority figure.

However, the whole New Testament, not just the pastoral epistles, should be our model on the question of bestowing authority. Different needs at different times and locations resulted in three unique patterns. In Jerusalem the need for quick, definite, clear cut decisions led to authority given predominantly by individuals. In the Pauline epistles the need for community building resulted in the predominance of authority given by the community. In the later church the need for stability and rootedness produced an authority bestowed primarily by the tradition which we now know as Scripture. Although each of the three vehicles are always present to some degree at any given time, one can conclude that the needs of a particular time should determine which one ought to be predominant.

Role of Church Leadership

The pastoral epistles also give us an outline of those particular functions which the church ought to include at any stage in the development of leadership roles. Only in the case of the term "shepherd," do we have to go outside the pastoral epistles for one of the basic functions. Though the author of the pastorals never applied this name to church leaders, it was used at all stages of the developmental process and is the basis for our term, "pastor." Therefore, this shepherding function is essential to any examination of the role. Alongside this shepherding, the pastorals do provide us with three other intrinsic functions: overseer, elder, and teacher. The author of these epistles has intertwined all three of these terms, making it clear that each was basic to the functioning of church leaders. He occasionally used two other terms, prophet and evangelist, to describe the function of some of these persons. Yet their distinction from the role of teacher is not that

18

great. Because of this, as well as their infrequent use, it is fitting to treat them as part of the overall teaching ministry. The only other official term used in the pastorals was "deacon," which clearly designated a non-pastoral office of lesser authority. Apostles are non-existent in these epistles, having previously disappeared from the life of the church. Therefore, one should not build a conception of leadership function around them, even though they influenced the development of the other functions and often served as a source of authority. Thus we have four primary functions -- shepherding, eldership, overseeing, and teaching -- which should become the building blocks of a church leadership role during any age.

However, the New Testament does not give us any precedent to follow in determining which function should predominate and serve as a focus for the whole role. Both eastern and western churches focused their conceptions around that function which had originated with each tradition respectively. The western church named the office "overseer" (pastoral epistles); whereas the eastern churches named the office, "elder" (James). One should expect this in such an early stage of development, but it does not serve to set any guidelines for the later church. The particular needs of each age must become the determining factor.

NOTES

1.   Hans Kung, <u>The Church</u>, trans. by Ray and Rosaleen Ockenden (New York: Sheed and Ward, 1967), pp. 363, 388-390.

2.   Karl H. Rengstorf, "ἀποστέλλω, ἐξαποστέλλω, ἀπόστολος, ψευδαπόστολος, ἀποστολή," in <u>Theological Dictionary of the New Testament</u>, ed. by Gerhard Kittel, trans. by Geoffrey W. Bromiley, Vol. I (Grand Rapids: William B. Eerdmans Pub. Co., 1964), pp. 430-437.

3.   Hans von Campenhausen, <u>Ecclesiastical Authority and Spiritual Power In The Church of The First Three Centuries</u>, trans. by J. A. Baker (Stanford, California: Stanford University Press, 1969), p. 27.

4.   Kung, pp. 348-353.

5.   Ernst Kaesemann, <u>Essays On New Testament Themes</u>, trans. by W. J. Montague (Naperville, Illinois: Alec R. Allenson, Inc., 1964), p. 86.

6.   Gunther Bornkamm, "πρέσβυς, πρεσβύτερος, πρεσβύτης, συμπρεσβύτερος, πρεσβυτέριον, πρεσβέυω," in <u>Theological Dictionary of the New Testament</u>, ed. by Gerhard Kittel, trans. by Geoffrey W. Bromiley, vol. VI (Grand Rapids: William B. Eerdmans Pub. Co., 1968), pp. 660-663.

7.   Burton Scott Easton, <u>The Pastoral Epistles</u> (New York: Charles Scribner's Sons, 1947), pp. 191-194.

8.   Burnett H. Streeter, <u>The Primitive Church</u> (London: MacMillan and Co., 1929), p. 40.

9.   Easton, p. 226.

10.   Joachim Jeremias, "ποιμήν, ἀρχιποίμην, ποιμαίνω, ποίμνη, ποίμνιον," in <u>Theological Dictionary of the New Testament</u>, ed. by Gerhard Kittel, translated by Geoffrey W. Bromiley, Vol. VI (Grand Rapids: William B. Eerdmans Pub. Co., 1968), p. 489.

20

11. Easton, p. 193.

12. Kung, p. 406.

13. Bornkamm, p. 664.

14. Kaesemann, p. 64.

15. Campenhausen, pp. 33-38.

16. Eduard Schweizer, Church Order In The New Testament, trans. by Frank Clarke (Naperville, Illinois: Alec R. Allenson, Inc., 1961), p. 194.

17. Kung, pp. 396-397.

18. Campenhausen, p. 65.

19. Kung, pp. 398-399, 402.

20. Easton, p. 224.

21. Campenhausen, p. 68.

22. Hermann W. Beyer, "ἐπισκέπτομαι, ἐπισκοπέω, ἐπισκοπή, ἐπίσκοπος, ἀλλοτριεπίσκοπος," in Theological Dictionary of the New Testament, ed. by Gerhard Kittel, trans. by Geoffrey W. Bromiley, Vol. II (Grand Rapids: William B. Eerdmans Pub. Co., 1964), p. 616.

23. Campenhausen, p. 69.

24. Kung, p. 408.

25. Beyer, p. 616.

26. Campenhausen, pp. 84, 116.

27. Ibid., pp. 71-72.

28. Karl H. Rengstorf, "διδάσκω, διδάσκαλος, νομοδιδάσκαλος, καλοδιδάσκαλος, ψευδοδιδάσκαλος, διδασκαλία, ἑτεροδιδασκαλέω, διδαχή, διδακτός, διδακτικός" in Theological Dictionary of the New Testament, ed. by Gerhard Kittel, trans. by Geoffrey W. Bromiley, Vol. II (Grand Rapids: William B. Eerdmans Pub. Co., 1964), p. 158.

29. Jeremias, p. 497-498.

30. Schweizer, pp. 197-200.

31. Kung, p. 400.

32. Campenhausen, pp. 121-123.

33. Easton, p. 175.

34. Martin Dibelius and Hans Conzelmann, The Pastoral Epistles: A Commentary on the Pastoral Epistles, ed. by Helmut Koester, trans. by Philip Buttolph and Adela Yarbro (Philadelphia: Fortress Press, 1972), p. 56.

35. Kaesemann, pp. 86-88.

36. Campenhausen, pp. 117-118.

37. Ibid., pp. 1-2.

CHAPTER II

LEADERSHIP FUNCTIONS IN THE NEW TESTAMENT

The apostle Paul used the poignant image of a master builder (ἀρχιτέκτων) to describe the role of church leadership. Referring to himself and Apollos, he wrote, "We are God's fellow workers; . . . like a skilled master builder I laid the foundation and another man is building upon it." (1 Cor. 3:9-10). This master builder was an assistant architect, a working foreman, who could plan tasks for oneself, as well as for one's "fellow workers." The work of these coworkers was equally as important as one's own. The master builder worked with the crew on the job, even becoming their servant, rather than sitting behind a desk in an "air conditioned" office.[1] In the church, such master builders were certainly the equippers of the saints for the building up of the body of Christ. They worked alongside their people to train them, by example, to build up their fellowship and reach out in ministry to outsiders.

It is important now to consider the various functions by which these master builders equipped the saints: shepherding, eldership, overseeing, and teaching. One can discover the unique quality of each name by examining its derivation, as well as its use during the first century. Careful scrutiny will reveal that the original, primary influence on most of them was secular. The early church borrowed greatly from the secular world to find adequate conceptions of leadership functions. Where they did utilize fundamentally religious terms, these, in turn, had largely secular origins. The secular sources of Biblical understandings lend support, then, to the utilization of secular models for the contemporary development of church leadership roles. Finally, the way the early church modified the meanings of these secular functions is significant. They selectively and purposely emphasized certain elements of the meaning of each term in order to fit their unique needs as a church.

Shepherding

Hebrew Usage

The shepherd imagery apparently enjoyed widespread use as a description of both religious and secular callings in the ancient world. Nowhere did anyone appoint, through official channels, a special group of people to an office called "shepherd." Instead they applied the designation to other official persons as a descriptive image. The Qumran community used it to delineate the tasks of authoritative overseers.[2]   Philo compared the task of shepherding a flock to leading the nation.   He even proposed it as good preparation for a ruler.   Yet, the early church undoubtedly took this concept primarily from later Judaism. It used the image to characterize any occupation with a great potential for caring, especially leaders and teachers.   Thus, the predominant source of meaning came from the Hebrew people and their Old Testament Scriptures.[3]

However, one should not mistakenly assume that this was primarily a religious designation.   In addition to its use by the Hebrews to describe secular callings, the term derived originally from the secular task of tending the flocks.   Though the image did carry religious connotations, ancient people throughout the Near East often applied it to secular officials.   The Sumerians called their king a shepherd. The Babylonian and Assyrian kings used it to describe themselves as the divine carriers of salvation. Righteous government, the gathering of the dispersed, and care for the weak were, in their eyes, the marks of this function.[4]   Since "righteous government" hardly pertains to sheep, modification of the original meaning had clearly taken place already. In fact, the moment someone used the term as an image, they modified its meaning.   Caring for persons was different from caring for animals.

In the Old Testament, one finds most of the shepherd (רֹעֶה) terminology in the prophets, indicating its late addition to the Hebrew vocabulary.   The Hebrews probably borrowed the term from the other older civilizations around them.   Like their predecessors, they commonly understood the term to mean rule (Is. 44:28), utilizing the image to describe both political and military leaders (1 Sam. 21:18, 2 Sam. 7:7)[5] They saw these leaders as God's delegates, vested with God's authority.[6]   Yet, unlike the Babylonians and

24

Babylonians and Assyrians, these shepherds were not the bearers of salvation. God alone could be savior or chief shepherd. Thus, they further defined the shepherd imagery as it applied to human leaders.

Ezekiel described well the responsibility of the Hebrew shepherds by his criticism of those who were unfaithful.

> Ho, shepherds of Israel who have been feeding yourselves! Should not shepherds feed the sheep? You eat the fat, you clothe yourselves with the wool, you slaughter the fatlings; but you do not feed the sheep. The weak you have not strengthened, the sick you have not healed, the crippled you have not bound up, the strayed you have not brought back, the lost you have not sought, and with force and harshness you have ruled them.
>
> (34:2b-4)

Other Old Testament writers also wrote of the function of the shepherd. Isaiah told of the shepherd who would gather, carry, and gently lead the flock (Cha. 40), and of the watchman (shepherd) who would warn the flock. The psalmist pictured the shepherd restoring the soul and bringing comfort (Cha. 23). Jeremiah promised a shepherd who would feed with knowledge and understanding (Cha. 3), and spoke of his role in protecting the flock (Cha. 23). To Zechariah, the true shepherd knit the people together and protected them from false shepherds who neglected the healthy, treated the weak mercilessly, voraciously devoured the wealth of the flock, and neglected to care for them (Cha. 11).

New Testament Usage

To best discover the function of a New Testament shepherd one must look to our model par excellence, that Great Shepherd of the sheep. By describing himself (Jn. 10) Jesus indicated the shepherd should know the sheep well enough to call each one by name. Jesus demonstrated this himself, by seeking out and personally calling (gathering) his twelve disciples. These men certainly had opportunity to know and be known by him, while they lived and travelled together. Jesus must have observed very carefully their behavior, empathizing with the needs underlying their actions. As he did with so many others, he must have

25

healed, comforted and strengthened them. He fed them like a shepherd, both literally, as they picked corn in the fields, and symbolically, through his teaching. Furthermore he provided the ultimate feeding of bread and wine as he completely gave himself to his sheep. Consequently, when his sheep heard his voice, they trusted him and followed him, enabling him to go before and lead them. He had built the rapport necessary to correct and warn them when they departed from the way of his Father. Yet his protection was there even when they failed, as in Peter's attempt to walk on the water (Matt. 14:28-33). Finally Jesus showed concern that they be able to minister to one another as shepherds. In John 21, Jesus' charge to Peter was to feed and tend (ποίμαινε) the sheep.

This task of enabling others to be shepherds is reinforced by one of the few New Testament passages which speaks at all extensively of this function. 1 Peter 5:2-3 tells shepherds to, "tend the flock of God that is your charge, not by constraint but willingly, not for shameful gain but eagerly, not as domineering over those in your charge but being examples to the flock." This admonition to "be examples" demonstrates the need for the flock to take on the task of shepherding themselves. Other passages also indicate this. Paul many times exhorted his readers to: "Bear one another's burdens" (Gal. 6:2); "admonish one another in all wisdom" (Col. 3:16); and "Encourage one another and build one another up." (1 Thess. 5:11). Yet this mutual guidance of one another could never completely negate the need for the shepherd leader. James provided a good balance when he required confession of sins to one another (5:16), yet also told the sick to call for their shepherds (5:14). The shepherd who tried to do all the shepherding could find it an impossible task. Yet the leader, who avoided the task of shepherding, took away the example from the flock. He would then, in Ezekiel's words, be accountable for those who strayed (Ezek. 33).

Summary

The shepherd is, first, one who gets to know the flock. The shepherd cares, seeks out, feeds, comforts, strengthens, heals, defends and provides. He or she observes and attempts to identify with the people in order to understand them. Second, the shepherd leads and guides the sheep. Only after one has gained their trust can one protect, correct, and warn. Finally,

the shepherd encourages the flock to be this kind of
support for one another.

Eldership

Hebrew Usage

The term "elder" came primarily from Hebrew origins. Yet, as with the shepherd imagery, this does
not necessarily bring one to conclude an essentially
religious meaning. The word "elder" (זָקֵן) had a long
history as a title for both secular and religious
rulers of the people of Israel. Their existence went
back as far as recorded Hebrew history. In the burn-
ing bush God told Moses to go to the tribal councils,
called elders (Ex. 3:16). Centuries later, these same
elders were the ones who caused Jesus to suffer (Matt.
16:21). Moses inherited an elder structure which may
have existed throughout the exodus.[7] However, he
appears to have appointed an intertribal body of
elders to help him govern the people (Num. 11:16).
These seventy men did share the leadership with him,
yet could take no initiative themselves. Generally,
their domain was the secular. They were the representatives of, and witnesses on behalf of, the people
(Ex. 24:1). They were the upholders of the law and
acted as judges for the people. They were representatives of God, yet did not perform any sacral
functions. However, their role was not without any
religious significance, for the first thing they did
as elders was to prophesy in ecstacy. Hence, they
were political rulers with a spiritual character.

After the Israelite people had settled in Canaan,
the elders became the leading members of municipal
nobility. During normal times, they made most of the
secular decisions in political, military and judicial
matters.[8] But in times of trouble the people looked
for the appearance of a charismatic judge, mighty
man, or messenger of God. Eventually this pattern of
government, with elders and "mighty men of God" became
inadequate. It lacked the stability necessary for
political survival. Hence, the monarchy came into
existence and became dominant for many years.[9] However, the power of the elders was still great enough
to influence the kings. David made treaties with them
when they sided against him, first with Abner (2 Sam.
3:17) and then with Absalom (2 Sam. 17:4, 15). In
cases such as these, a national body, called the
Elders of Israel, appears to have existed (2 Sam.

3:17, 5:3). Undoubtedly, elders from districts and tribes met together periodically to make these common decisions (1 Sam. 30:26).[10]

During the exile, the elders became the heads of the community. With all other political forms shattered, they provided the only strong internal leadership. They were the ones to stand and bring to the people the message of the Lord (Jer. 26:17). The exile took away the opportunity to exercise extensive political control. Yet it created a greater need for a sense of tradition. Thus the religious replaced the secular as the focus of their modified function. Their most significant task became guarding and interpreting the tradition. By the time the Israelite people returned again to their own land, the structure of this body of elders also changed. Certain aristocratic families, called "father's houses," had totally replaced the tribal units.[11] Ezra appointed such a centralized body of elders to make judicial decisions affecting all the people (10:16). Thus, the change of political realities brought this judicial element back into greater prominence. Still, it did not diminish the important task of tradition bearing.

Through this historical development, one can see the secular and religious influences on the Judaism of New Testament times. The predominant meaning was still that of ruler. On the one hand, these ruler-elders held civil or criminal court, managed community property, assessed local taxes, and performed other governmental tasks. On the other hand, they also governed the synagogues by providing the necessities for service, though they did not actually lead the worship. Furthermore, the elders of the Great Sanhedrin had to have a precise knowledge of, and interpretation of, the law in order to correctly transmit the tradition.[12]

Gentile Usage

The Greeks and Egyptians used the term "elder." The constitution of Sparta included it as a political title to denote the president of a college. Greek society often used it in a non-official sense to refer to various kinds of senior groups, as distinct from junior ones. The Egyptians used it during the Ptolemaic and imperial periods as a title to describe a variety of committees and colleges. A guild of millers in Alexandria took it as a title, as did other corporations. Elders also appeared in village

28

government, functioning in administrative and judicial capacities. The Egyptians even used it as a title for the priests of the "great God Socnopaios."[13] Thus one can conclude that this title enjoyed widespread secular usage by the time of the New Testament.

Both Hebrew and Greek literature used the term "πρεσβύτερος" to also mean an older person, men of old, ancestors, traditions of the ancestors, or witness of events in the past. In addition to verifying the task of guarding the tradition, this imputed a kind of "wisdom of the ages" to one who held the title. In fact, the elder was one who personified the discerning ability of an old man as well as ancient and sacred traditions. Consequently, the term "elder" also embodied deep respect. Greek literature showed the degree of dignity given to the term by using it to represent glorified human beings, and even astral deities. [14] On a more human level later Judaism used it as an honorary title for the heads of leading families and the fathers and forefathers of the deceased.[15]

The New Testament Usage

The early church probably drew from Hebrew origins predominantly. In choosing the term "elder" rather than "chief priest," they selected a title not vested with great power. It is possible that they purposefully selected this title because it represented the lay membership of the Sanhedrin. Yet, they did make modifications in their use of the term. Some of the judicial and administrative functions of village government may have been inappropriate to the church context. Plus the church discarded the class requirement within the Sanhedrin. Privileged, aristocratic persons had no more rights than others to become elders. However, the Hebrew heritage did supply the basic outline of tasks. The elders in Jerusalem were the representatives of the people, receiving the gifts sent by the church in Antioch (Acts 11:30). In Ephesus they are addressed as guardians of the tradition, to whom is entrusted the guidance and protection of the community (Acts 20:17-38). In 1 Peter they have the power to discipline the church (5:3). James made them intercessors on behalf of the saints and representations of God's healing power (5:14). Timothy, probably an elder, was responsible for the public reading of Scripture (1 Tim. 4:13). 2 John and 3 John continue to ascribe the Hebrew connotations of honor and dignity to this title (verse 1 of each epistle).

Summary

This title carried very specific meanings when it described the leadership of the New Testament church. The elder was the ruler who exercised judgment and discipline. But most significantly, the elder was the authority figure who represented God to the people, the people to God, and the people to one another. As God's representative, the elder was the wise old person who would bring grace and healing to the sick. This one was the very personification of sacred tradition, who had been entrusted with its preservation, interpretation, and public proclamation. As the representative of the people, the elder came before God in intercessory prayer and acted toward other Christian groups on behalf of the home church. Finally, as a result of this title, the elder became the recipient of honor, dignity and respect.

Overseeing

Gentile Influence on New Testament Usage

The term "overseer" came primarily from Greek culture. It had wide secular usage as another word for ruler. The Greeks generally used the title to designate a superintendent who visited those he supervised.[16] Occasionally they used the word in a non-official sense to mean onlooker, watcher, protector, or patron. But the important meaning for the New Testament came from its official use.

Greek literature sometimes referred to the gods as overseers. These tutelary gods watched out for those under their care, fighting against other gods and powers on their behalf. The Greeks used "overseers" to address men and women in many different circumstances: the ship captain in charge of his ship, women designated to watch over young married couples, market superintendents who judged fair and improper dealings, and building contractors who supervised the men and controlled the money. The Athenians used this title for state officials whom they sent to govern cities subject to their control under the Attic League. These governors exercised some judicial powers, but their main responsibility was to preserve public order and avoid any friction with others.[17] Furthermore, the Greeks used this term to refer to watchmen, supervisors of slaves, and a variety of other persons.[18]

The early church certainly had in mind a similar function for their overseers. The church gave them regular responsibility for the care of the church (1 Tim. 3:5), church discipline (2 Tim. 2:25) and the oversight of the larger body of elders (1 Tim. 5:17-20). However, as has been mentioned, the master-builder of the early church was more than a dignitary who came and looked in to see if everything was all right. Like the secular overseer, one undoubtedly felt called to keep order in the community. But ideally this was not to be done by sweeping friction under the rug. In short, the early church seems to have modified the Greek concept of overseer, emphasizing one's responsibility to work with the laity on any given task.

The Cynic-Stoic philosophers added another sense to this term. An overseer became one who tested out another person to determine degree of conformity to the truth.[19] The early Christian overseers most certainly saw something similar in their task. When Paul perceived friction between Euodia and Syntyche in the Philippian church, he called for a yokefellow, probably an overseer, to help these women (Phil. 4:2-3). This yokefellow was probably one of the overseers addressed at the beginning of the letter. Certainly this yokefellow-overseer could not have helped unless he, himself, had accurately perceived the state of these women's lives.

Overseers also existed among the religious officials in Greek culture. Some religious cults referred to their journeying preachers as overseers.[20] More typically, as with the Society for Maintaining the Sanctuary of Apollo of Rhodes, they were responsible for financial transactions and other temporal tasks. These overseers, like those in the early church, did not perform cultic duties.[21] Presumably the Christian church purposely passed over the term used for the priest of these temples. Such a word would have destroyed the ministry of the priesthood of all believers. So they chose a title which would describe an authority figure with less cultic function. It is questionable to what extent the Christian overseers handled the finances, as did their pagan counterparts.

31

The author of the pastoral epistles warned them against becoming lovers of money (1 Tim. 3:2), and referred to them as God's Stewards (Tit. 1:7). Yet we never actually find them overseeing the financial affairs of the churches.

Hebrew Influence on New Testament Usage

There is some possibility of tracing the origins of the term "overseer" back to Judaism. Neither the synagogue rulers, nor the leaders of the Dead Sea Sects were called overseers.[22] Yet the leader (ἀρχισυνάγωγος) and assistant (ὑπηρέτης) of the synagogue might have been models for the Christian overseers and deacons respectively. In both cases a close connection existed between the two offices. The leader of the synagogue even had a group of elders surrounding him. His task was to conduct divine worship, supervise the external order, and look after the building. If the church did use the synagogue as a model in this manner, they definitely modified the function. The leader of the synagogue had little to do with the guidance of the congregation as a fellowship of faith and love, a task central to the Christian overseer. Plus the synagogue leader probably had more cultic functions than did the overseers of the New Testament period.

Another possible model existed in the leaders of the Community of the New Covenant in Damascus. This pharisaical community had an overseer (מְבַקֵּר) at the head of each camp, but never cited other office bearers, such as deacon. The overseer had charge of admitting, examining, correcting, and expelling people. He convened and directed the assemblies of the community. He received and distributed the offerings. He had judicial responsibility and authority over many external things. He was a teacher and preacher, and had the power to pardon sins. It is questionable whether such a small community in Damascus could have become a direct model for the whole Christian church.[23] Yet, Paul's pharisaical ties with Damascus could have acquainted him with this community. If Paul and others did use this model, they probably modified it even more than the synagogue model. Paul's emphasis on charismatic authority would seem to necessitate stripping the overseer of most of the monarchical power and authority given him by the Pharisees.

32

Finally, the early church could have taken this term from the Septuagint. This Greek translation of the Old Testament used ἐπίσκοπος as a description for persons with both secular and religious responsibilities. These translators used this term to describe: officers of the army (2 Kings 11:15, 18), civil officers (Neh. 11:9, 14 and Is. 60:17), overseers of workmen (2 Chron. 34:12, 17) and priests (Num. 4:16 and Jer. 20:1).[24]

Summary

Whatever the source of meaning, the primary tasks of the New Testament overseer are clear. As the Christian church took and modified this title, they found themselves with a ruler who acted as manager, supervisor, director, superintendent, and guardian (as the word is translated in 1 Pet. 2:25). This overseer was responsible for the care of the church as a whole, as well as the supervision of the ministry of individual members. The task was to keep the church in order and give it guidance. It was to watch over, judge, and discipline when necessary. Yet it was not permissible to stay "on the bench" while the team dug in for the dirty work. Instead this was a "playing coach." An effective coach needed to actively examine the operation of the entire team and the condition of each member. The overseer had to watch for potential crises, and then be capable of responding appropriately.

Teaching

The broadest conception of the teaching function of the New Testament includes a number of specifically designated ministries. In addition to the New Testament teacher (διδάσκαλος), we must briefly examine, under this category, two other ministries, prophet (προφήτης) and evangelist (εὐαγγελιστής). The term "teacher" had roots in both Greek and Hebrew culture; the word "prophet" came primarily from the Hebrews, and "evangelist" only from the Greeks.

Gentile Usage

The Greeks used the word "teacher" to refer to school masters and choirmasters. The school master was a teacher of definite skills such as reading, fighting, or music. The teaching of skills must have been important to the New Testament teacher who had

33

the responsibility of equipping individuals for the
work of ministry. Thus, the school master model would
have been useful, despite the unique nature of skills
needed in the church. The choirmaster practiced with,
and trained, the chorus that sang during a theater
performance in which he, himself, was an actor.[25]
This was also a particularly useful model, illustra-
ting the possibilities for joint, leader-pupil under-
takings. This was very similar to Paul's image of the
master builder with his fellow workers. Yet, the
early Christians had to modify the choirmaster and
school master images to allow for the less structured
church situations. The church leader did not always
perform alongside one's people according to very
precise cues. Nor was there always the formal setting
of classroom or tutoring. Plus the different subject
matter necessitated special capabilities on the part
of teachers and distinct responses on the part of
students.

In Greek literature, an evangelist was, "one who
proclaimed oracular sayings."[26] This "town crier"
function was a simpler, yet similar, task to the New
Testament evangelist. The Christian evangelist, like
the secular counterpart, concentrated on proclaiming
the message to those who had not heard (2 Cor. 10:16).
However, the message of the Christian, in contrast to
the secular, evangelist was always basically the same,
a gospel of good news. Furthermore, this gospel demanded a response. Consequently, the Christian
evangelist, unlike the secular, would spend time with
an individual who needed further explanation. Finally, the Christian conception of this task sometimes
included writing down the proclamation. The message
was so important that four separate evangelists under-
took the task of recording the story.

Hebrew and New Testament Usage

The teachers of the New Testament derived a good
deal of their meaning from the teacher (חָכָם) of later
Judaism, despite the infrequent use of διδάσκαλος in
the Septuagint. One can see the Judaic derivation by
looking at Jesus, the prime example of New Testament
teaching. His contemporaries often addressed him by
the term "rabbi." Moreover, he used the rabbinic pattern of a teacher-pupil relationship to describe his
own relationship to his disciples (Matt. 10:24-
25).[27]

In addition to the designation, "rabbi," Judaism used the honorary title, "scribe" (סֵפֶר), to refer to a select portion of the teachers.[28] This special group, as well as the other teachers, had a long history. The scribes existed at least as far back as David (2 Sam. 8:17) and included important figures like Ezra (Ezra 7:21). The predecessor of all rabbis, including the scribes, was the wise man (חָכָם). Although the record only mentions a few such persons by name, most notably Solomon, they held a respected and important position.

The prophets of the New Testament also came from Judaism and the Hebrew tradition. One can see the link in the person of John the Baptist. This forerunner of the New Testament was a continuation of a line that began with the early Hebrew prophet (נָבִיא) and seer (הֹזֶה). These prophets may date back as far as the prophesying of the elders of Israel after their appointment by Moses (Num. 11:25).

The basic character of these teachers and prophets remained constant from the earliest beginnings through the New Testament period. However, their purposes, their styles, and the settings in which they functioned, did change from one age to another. Thus, New Testament teaching was a modified function even apart from its Greek origins. To appreciate these modifications of the Hebrew background, it is important to understand the development of the purposes, the styles, and the settings of teaching and prophecy.

The Purpose

Communicating the Word of God was the essential task of both the teachers and prophets throughout the whole Biblical record. Both were concerned with reverence for God and justice for humankind.

The teacher of the Old Testament had a similar responsibility to the elder, since the wise man (חָכָם) was a larger designation that included the elder or scribe (סֵפֶר). The primary task of these wise men was to interpret the Torah.[29] They used the past revelation of God to perceive the working of the Spirit in the contemporary situation. Their job was to inculcate faith in God and clarify correct conduct. These educators of conscience often provided daily instruction on a broad spectrum of issues. They were especially concerned for the faithful execution of responsibilities by those in a position of authority, such as parents.[30] Furthermore, they had a concern for the integrity and personal growth of the individual, encouraging each person to seek one's own counsel and find one's own direction. To some degree this task of educating the conscience overlapped with what subsequent generations would call the secular domain.

In contrast, the Old Testament prophet was a spokesperson of direct revelation from God (Deut. 18:18). Furthermore, the later Old Testament prophets performed functions that following generations would see as even more secular in nature than their wise men counterparts. They helped solve domestic national problems (1 Sam. 9:7f.), intervened in political issues (1 Ki. 11:29ff; 14:1f.), and officially performed certain political and military responsibilities (1 Ki. 20:13f.). Nathan, as a resident prophet in the court of David, sometimes functioned more like a modern political advisor than a contemporary religious figure.

The New Testament prophets greatly modified the balance of religious and political concerns. They did not often address the rulers on political matters. Instead, they were primarily preachers of the Word of Christ. Like their predecessors, they usually spoke the direct revelation of God to a particular concrete situation in either the present or the future. But the purpose was the edification of the church and its members, rather than all of society. They could speak words of consolation and encouragement or call for repentance, depending on the need at the time (1 Cor. 14:3-12).[31]

The New Testament teachers also preached the word of Christ for both present and future situations. However, unlike their prophetic contemporaries, the teachers were more in debt to tradition. Their task was to interpret the Old Testament in the light of the young church and pass on the developing tradition surrounding the message of Jesus Christ. Like the Hebrew wise men, they were masters of instruction who handed on the precepts and propositions of the faith and applied them to contemporary needs. Like the ancient scribes, they addressed the need to love both God and humankind, and sought to instill right conduct through "sound teachings." Undoubtedly, this manner of instruction was familiar to the early Christian teachers through their contact with the rabbis and scribes of later Judaism. The professed purpose of these Judaic teachers of the law was, "to show the way of God from the Torah and maintain a tradition of Scripture readings and teachings from generation to generation."[32] However, according to Jesus (Matt. 23) they had corrupted the practice by lending more weight to their own decisions than to the Torah itself. Thus the early Christian teachers saw themselves as the true descendants of the Old Testament wise men.

The Style

The styles of teachers and prophets were distinct throughout the Biblical period. Both Old and New Testament teachers sought to expound systematically the Scripture and tradition. The prophets of both testaments were innovative and intuitive in their preaching. Yet historical development in their modes of action does occur.

The earliest prophets were ecstatic visionaries, often described as "mad fellows." Yet, the later Old Testament prophets seldom behaved in this manner. They preached comprehensively and responsibly, instead of appearing to be out of touch with the world around them. The New Testament prophets patterned themselves after the latter variety, as Paul demonstrated by commending their levelheadedness (1 Cor. 14).

Both the prophets[33] and teachers in the New Testament adopted an analogical style. The teachers may well have copied the parabolic style of Jesus, a much looser format than the rabbinic method of instruction. Although Jesus could effectively use the "question-answer" approach, he felt no obligation to adhere strictly to such a cold, rigid form of teaching. The early church undoubtedly shared this relative sense of freedom in their teaching.

The Old Testament provided another good model for a balance between structure and freedom. The Old Testament wise men relied on argument and reasoned admonition in their counseling. They gave structured lessons on subjects such as prayer. Yet, they were extremely creative, warm, and intimate in their writings, to which the Psalms and Proverbs attest. The author(s) of the Proverbs frequently spoke in the motif of a "father-son" relationship, giving a continual impression of intimacy and warm concern.[34] Nothing in Scripture is more representative of creative freedom than the Psalms, of which the wise men,

37

Heman and Ethan, wrote at least two, Ps. 88 and Ps. 89 respectively. The presence of the term מַשְׂכִּיל in the heading of each of these Psalms means they were "a set of verses used for instruction."

Despite the similarities to the wise men, the New Testament teachers modified even this model in at least one significant way. They copied Jesus' method of discipling, a much more intense relationship than the discipling entered into by some Old Testament prophets and some rabbis of later Judaism. The author of 2 Tim. probably referred to this form of teaching when he directed Timothy to, "entrust to faithful men who will be able to teach others also" (2:2). The early Christian teachers must have observed how their Lord became a facilitator, enabler, stimulator, and resource person for many different people.

The Setting

Finally, the settings in which teaching and prophecy took place, also changed. The Old Testament prophets regularly spoke to the entire public, often moving around from place to place. Conversely, their New Testament counterparts primarily served one local church. This same modification occurred with the teachers. The primary place of instruction for the wise men was, "in the street, in the markets . . . ; on the top of the walls . . . ; at the entrance of the city gates." (Prov. 1:20-21). The teachers of later Judaism modified this, to some extent, by functioning only within their own local synagogue.[35] Then, Jesus further changed the Old Testament pattern by spending even more time with individuals and a small group of disciples than he did with large crowds. The teachers of the early church continued both of these modifications. They frequently worked with individuals and small groups and stayed usually within one local congregation.

Summary

The teaching function of the New Testament involved equipping the saints for the work of ministry and building up the body of Christ. To assist in building up the church, they gave instruction in faith and conduct, support through consolation and encouragement, and a challenge to grow and mature. To develop a corps of ministers, they called and empowered believers to continue the mission of Jesus Christ, to find direction for their lives, and to

38

develop the necessary skills for their ministries. They needed to be open to God's direction in their own lives in order to accomplish these tasks. Sometimes they worked in highly structured situations, like expounding the Scriptures or preparing lessons. Other times they found themselves in a free and open atmosphere, as in discipling another person or the spontaneous preaching of the gospel. Finally, they found it advantageous to work in large group, small group, and individual settings, depending on circumstances. In short, the teacher became instructor of the faith, stimulator of the body of Christ, trainer of skills, enabler of individuals, facilitator of groups, preacher to the many, and resource person for all.

1. W.T. Purkiser, _The New Testament Image of the Ministry_ (Kansas City, Missouri: Beacon Hill Press of Kansas City, 1969), p. 40.

2. Raymond E. Brown, _The Gospel According To John (XIII-XXI)_, Vol. 29:2 of _The Anchor Bible_, ed. by William F. Albright and David N. Freedman (Garden City, New York: Doubleday and Co., Inc., 1970), p. 1114.

3. Jeremias, pp. 488-490.

4. _Ibid._, p. 486.

5. _Ibid._, p. 488.

6. Brown, p. 1114.

7. Bornkamm, p. 655.

8. _Ibid._, p. 656.

9. Yehezkel Kaufmann, _The Religion of Israel_, trans. and abridged by Moshe Greenberg (Chicago: University of Chicago Press, 1960), pp. 256-262.

10. Bornkamm, p. 657.

11. _Ibid._, p. 658.

12. Easton, pp. 191-192.

13. Bornkamm, p. 653.

14. Walter Bauer, _A Greek-English Lexicon of the New Testament and Other Early Christian Literature_, trans. and adapted by William F. Arndt and F. Wilbur Gringrich (Chicago: University of Chicago Press, 1957), pp. 706-707.

15. Bornkamm, p. 661.

16. Bauer, p. 299.

17. Beyer, pp. 609-611.

18. Kung, p. 399.

19. Beyer, p. 611.

20. Kung, p. 399.

21. Beyer, pp. 612-613.

22. Ibid., p. 407.

23. Ibid., pp. 618-619.

24. Easton, p. 222.

25. Rengstorf, Vol. I, pp. 148-149.

26. Gerhard Friedrich, "εὐαγγελίζομαι, εὐαγ-γέλιον, προευαγγελίζομαι, εὐαγγελιστής," in Theological Dictionary of the New Testament, ed. by Gerhard Kittel, trans. by Geoffrey W. Bromiley, Vol. II (Grand Rapids: William B. Eerdmans Pub. Co., 1964), pp. 736-737.

27. Rengstorf, Vol. II, pp. 151-152.

28. Bornkamm, p. 660.

29. Rengstorf, Op. Cit., p. 153.

30. John T. McNeill, A History of The Cure of Souls (New York: Harper and Brothers Publishers, 1951), pp. 9-11.

31. Kung, p. 396.

32. Ibid., p. 397.

33. Ibid., pp. 396-397.

34. McNeill, pp. 9-11.

35. Rengstorf, Vol. II, p. 152.

CHAPTER III

ROLE AND AUTHORITY IN CHURCH HISTORY

It is important now to examine the history of the church in order to better understand the relationship between the four church leadership functions during both healthy and unhealthy periods. It is also important to investigate the interrelation of the three possible sources of authority (individual, church, and Scripture) during the same given times. Effective leadership necessitates the presence of all four functions and the recognition of all three sources of authority. Furthermore, in each case, one of these needs to be predominant, determined by the basic need of the age. Whenever this balance is upset, the performance of the ministry of both clergy and laity is less than satisfying and corrective action is needed. Specifically, an imbalance results in both the multiple, yet single-headed, leadership style and the charismatic/official bases of authority. Domination without accountability is often the product of losing a plurality of leadership and a sense of charismatic authority. Indecision and disorder are the likely consequences of neither designating a single head person nor accepting official authority. Both of these problems, along with others, are present in the three time periods to be examined. These periods include: 1) the age of the later Church Fathers, 2) the high middle ages, and 3) the Reformation. In each case, the point of entry, as well as the time period itself, can provide needed insight into the problems inherent in moving from a transition stage into a new focus.

To assist in determining the emerging foci for each age, one can observe signs in both ecclesiastical and secular domains. The place the congregation worships, and the place the pastor does the most work, tell us much about what is central in the ministry of pastor and church.[1] Secular roles and dominant patterns of authority are reflected in the primary function and source of authority for the church leadership of the same era. Finally, there should be an obvious connection between predominant function and source of authority during each period of church history.

The Age Of The Later Church Fathers

Basic Need

The time from Irenaeus to the Council of Nicea (ca. 180-325) represents a very different time than the first century. It was a time of tumultuous change, including: the decline of the Roman Empire and corruption of its leadership, increased persecution of the church, development of heresies such as Gnosticism and Montanism, and the influx of pagans into the church.[2] Thus the need arose to control and unify the church, to sustain its members, and to maintain a sense of order. In short, the church needed an authority figure who could provide these in one's very person.

Predominant Function

The need for an authority figure, a personification of that which is sacred, points to the predominance of eldership. Though the most commonly used title during this period was "bishop," close investigation shows the functioning to be more like eldership than oversight, in the New Testament sense of the terms. Hippolytus illustrated this confusing trend by his reference to the bishop as a high priest, a term laden with connotations of authority and personification of the sacred (Apostolic Tradition III). The bishop had, in fact, become Christ to the people, "the man" of the church.[3] Under the bishop a college of ordained presbyters assisted in the rule of the church. The central task of these clergy, the celebration of the eucharist, further indicated their function as symbolic authority figures. As celebrants of the eucharist, they were representatives of God through whom the worshipers experienced the Lord. Another sign of the predominance of eldership was the existence of the first church buildings. The fact that the people were willing to leave an intimate home environment for a larger place of worship showed their concern to improve the bishop's control over the whole church. Thus the very presence of these buildings indicated the church's desire for a strong central authority figure.[4]

This universal focus on eldership, centered in the title, "bishop," developed rather quickly. The former Palestinian function of elder became predominant within the developing gentile structure of one bishop over a number of elders. The dominance of

44

the eldership function was a consequence of the increasing need for authority. The ascendance of the
gentile structure resulted from the scattering of
Palestinian Christians after the Jewish revolts of 70
and 132-135.[5] Thus did the title, "bishop," come to
embody the eldership function even more than the
title, "presbyter."

Predominant Source of Authority

When the elder became the focal point of the
pastoral function, this authority figure naturally
became the primary bestower of authority to others.
The same basic need underlaid both function and source
of authority. A sole bishop could act quickly and
decisively to bring needed direction, control, order
and unity to the church. Irenaeus demonstrated this
by his use of apostolic succession, a line of authoritative individuals, to validate the accuracy of
"Catholic" teaching. To him the bishop was like the
banker of a bank (the church) into which Christ had
deposited his teaching (Heresies 3.4.1 and 4.26.2).
The figurehead position of the bishops naturally made
them the source of authority for the other more
numerous clergy under their supervision.[6] Not only
did they personally choose the presbyters and "lower
clergy" (Cyprian, Letters 23-29, 33-39:5, 34-40),
these others were extensions of their authority, who
could do nothing without their consent.[7] Only the
selection of the bishop necessitated the participation
of a group of laity and fellow bishops (Cyprian,
Letters 51-55:8; 66-68:2; 67:4,5). One symbol of the
relationship between bishop and presbyters was their
seating arrangement during worship. Like Jesus and
his disciples at the Last Supper, the bishop sat
behind the center of the eucharistic table, commissioning the presbyters on either side.[8]

The individual as a primary source of authority
was a marked change from the late New Testament period
where the scriptural tradition was predominant. This
focus shifted during the second century when the
growing and developing tradition became more complex.
More books, as well as more interpretations and
understandings, produced controversy and confusion.
Various church leaders, including the heretic Marcion,
prepared lists of canonical books. All this chaos
forced the church to find a clearer, more precise
source of authority. Thus, before the canon neared
completion by the end of the second century,[9] the
bishop filled this vacuum. We can see the rapidity of

this development in Clement of Rome, who originally traced the succession of apostles (93-97), and in Ignatius who admonished that no one should do anything without the bishop (letter to Smyrna) who represented Jesus Christ ([Ignatius to] Eph. 3:2) and God, himself (Magnesians 3:1). By the middle of the second century, Clement's apostolic succession had combined with Ignatius' monarchical bishop. Thus, the church had already established its prime source of authority elsewhere by the time it finally canonized the Scriptures.

Secular Parallels

To some degree the church consciously used the secular society of that time as a model for developing its predominant function and source of authority. In the Byzantine Empire the church gave bishops secular titles, insignias and privileges which had previously been reserved for the emperor or other high officials. Among these were candles, incense, a throne, shoes, the maniple, and the pallium.[10]

The western church equated the bishop with Caesar.[11] Furthermore, they used the term, "κλῆρος" (latin "ordo"), a common expression for orders of government dignitaries, to distinguish clergy from laity.[12] These clergy also assumed the titles of "prefect" and "vicar," originally names of magistrates within the empire. Moreover, the emperor, who was the divine ruler, the elder "par excellence," also became the sole source of law and authority. By late in the third century, he could name his successor, as well as his subordinates, who in turn could appoint those under them.[13]

Other Functions

The functions of shepherding, teaching, and overseeing were all still present in the third century church, though some were stronger than others. Shepherding was the strongest, due largely to the persecutions. Guiding people who faced difficult questions, sustaining them in courage and faith, and healing those who suffered injury were all essential tasks. Most important, however, was the reconciling of those who had compromised the faith with those who had remained steadfast. Many factions within the church held differing opinions on the degree and kind of renunciation forgivable.[14] Coupled with reconciling was the task of disciplining, or punishing, the

46

lapsed for their particular sin. Finally, this shepherd needed to care for the downtrodden and forgotten, particularly the aged, as well as those whom the persecutions left orphans and widows, poor or infirm.[15]

The teaching function was significant because the bases of faith and practice needed to be both delineated and taught. Thus, these teachers used philosophical, as well as catechetical, forms[16] to develop and interpret church discipline, the scriptural canon, apostolic doctrine, and credal formulations.[17] The central purpose of all teaching was the establishment of control over, and unity within, the church.

Overseeing, the weakest of the functions, frequently landed in the lap of whoever would do it. The bishop often passed the task of administration to the reluctant presbyters.[18] Though shepherding of individuals was important, supervising their ministries was not. This neglect was one of the most serious mistakes of the third century clergy. Only the guardianship of the whole church was a task that appealed to those whose prime concerns were the control and unity of the church.

Other Sources of Authority

The remaining two sources of authority also influenced the clergy of this period, though the church had greater significance than the Scripture. We can see the church's authority in the selection of bishops. Both the local congregation and other bishops, representing the larger church, played an important role. Occasionally, the local church even initiated a nomination. Yet their power was diminishing, as church leaders discouraged this procedure. On the other hand, the bishops were gaining power in the selection of a fellow bishop.[19] This ascendance of the church hierarchy represented quite a change from the first century congregation which could declare its own bishop. Though the local congregation continued to decline into the fourth century,[20] the church in its entirety remained an important source of authority. Again the need for unity and control determined that the hierarchical form of church authority would be the one to prevail.

The Scripture was also a source of authority, as we can see by the presence of "readers" among the "lower clergy." These readers of the Scripture lesson

47

were originally the most prominent of the minor officials.[21] Their demise indicated the decreasing, yet still present, influence of the Scripture. When the church did turn to the Scriptures, it used them primarily as a basis for developing apostolic doctrine and credal statements, as well as codifying church discipline. Once more, the purpose was for the unity, order, and control of the church.

Other Effects on Pastoral Authority and Lay Ministry

The demise of the overseeing function, as well as the Scripture and local church as sources of authority, was a problematic trend. It gave more control to the bishops and less to others. The church did need a great deal of this control in order to survive. Yet, the magnitude of their power stifled the ministry of the laity, the charismatic basis of authority, and the plurality of leadership.

Due to the character often produced through persecution, the church undoubtedly produced many fine lay ministers. Yet it had replaced the priesthood of all believers, the very basis of this ministry, with a select group of persons who were beginning to claim special relationship to God on the basis of their office. Increasingly they were the ones through whom God spoke and provided well-being. More and more it became their rituals which provided the very access to God.[22]

Vestiges of the charismatic basis of authority still existed, but they were on the decline. The charismatic order of teachers had disappeared.[23] Other charismatic activities, such as exorcism and healing, had now taken on an official character. We have already noted the decline of readers, who were chosen on the basis of moral performance and the ability to read, a rarity at that time. One glimpse of the charismatic appeared in the view that steadfast endurance of persecution was a manifestation of the Spirit, bringing with it the power to remit sins. The church actually recognized some of these "confessors" as presbyters, though this practice did not last long. Cyprian stated the prevailing mood when he claimed that a clergyman lost all power to minister if he forfeited his office by breaking communion with the Great Church. Even the prayers of such a clergyman could not usher in the grace of God.[24]

The plurality of leadership also began to break down with the increasing power of the bishop. When the bishopric became associated with a diocese, during the third century,[25] the gap widened further. The bishop was now the sole leader of the larger, more powerful diocese, whereas the presbyters had charge of the less powerful local congregations. This general loss of power on the part of the majority of the church was very slow and subtle, even understandable. Yet it began a process which eventually led to a major distortion of the gospel of Christ and the purpose of the church.

Conclusions

The early church leader had the momentous task of charting the direction for an infant church during very unstable times. Thus the emphasis on eldership plus individual and official authority was both necessary and important. Yet it is regrettable that this all-consuming task of establishing the church and the pastorate seemed to prohibit the development of other aspects of leadership role and authority, as well as the ministry of the laity. For, though it was difficult for them to realize, they needed an overseer-bishop with an appreciation for the charisma that God gives to individuals for the purpose of strengthening the local congregation. They needed someone who could perceive the potential for unity in a cooperative ministry of the total body of Christ, one who could have encouraged and supervised the ministry of the laity, even looking for gifts present in the church. If such an overseer could have actively included the presbyters and lower clergy in the leadership of the total church, they could have benefited greatly. Finally, a higher regard for the Scripture could also have helped these bishops perceive the more hidden needs. Yet their disregard for the parts which seemed strange to them is again, understandable. The possibility of being blinded by our own perspectives is always present.

The High Middle Ages

Basic Need

The two hundred year period following the middle of the eleventh century was a time of rapid growth and change. The world was emerging out of the Dark Ages with the beginnings of commerce, education, the middle

class, towns and cities. It was still the era of
feudalism, also the age of the Crusades and the Inquisition. Furthermore, the church was gaining in power
and influence. Yet the ravages of war, floods,
famine, disease, migration, avarice and brutality made
it a very uncertain world in which to live. Thus, the
basic need of this age was relief and escape from the
surrounding perils, care and comfort in the face of
tragedy, guidance and hope for both daily and eternal
existence.[26]

Predominant Function

Shepherding was the function most suited to
predominate in this kind of world, as the primary
tasks of the clergy illustrate. The church developed
a very detailed sacramental system, administered by
the clergy and designed to bring relief to any kind of
ill. The church instituted sacraments for the crisis
points of life: baptism for birth, matrimony for
marriage, extreme unction for death. In addition the
sacrament of penance offered relief at the very point
of sin and the Mass provided grace whenever and
whatever the need.[27] The Mass had developed into a
meritorious act which forced God to be gracious. One
could gain specific grace for either oneself or others
in any stated circumstance.[28] Penance, or the
exercise of authority over souls, grew out of the
church discipline of earlier times. A stiff penalty,
specifically designed for a certain sin, was to help
the penitent escape the kingdom of darkness and find
the kingdom of light. Pastors spent much time hearing
confessions and administering these penalties for the
salvation of souls. For, by the twelfth century,
everyone was required to confess before the
priest.[29] Healing was another essential caring task
of the clergy. Divine grace to heal body and spirit
was the promise of the clergy who had studied well the
manual of diagnoses and remedies. Charismatic healers
could be found. But it was more likely to be a common
priest who used saints, relics, exorcism, or oil for
anointing.[30] Finally, every priest was to take very
seriously the ministry of caring, as codified in the
seven corporal acts of mercy. These included: feeding the poor, giving drink to the thirsty, clothing
the naked, sheltering the homeless, visiting the sick,
ransoming the captive, and burying the dead.[31]

The local priest's main task was to hear confessions and give penance. The entire open church was

used as a confessional as well as a place of worship.[32] A stark contrast to the noisy world outside, this peaceful, dimly lit haven suggested the presence of the Great Shepherd. The high roofs and pointed arches demonstrated the majesty of God's power, while the statues of saints, angels and holy family looked down with God's protective care. The centrality of the altar and the eucharist completed the symbolization of grace that came to the penitent worshiper through the appointed shepherd in the name of the Great One who watched over all.[33]

The transition from eldership to shepherding took place a number of centuries prior to the High Middle Ages. We can see from the writings of Gregory the Great (590-604) that it was already predominant then. He instructed the governor of souls to care for various personalities, examining different treatments for each malady.[34] Undoubtedly the transition took place in response to the changed relationship of church and state, as well as the decline of the latter. From the time that Constantine inaugurated Christianity as the state religion (312) until the last Roman Emperor fell (476),[35] the church was catapulted from obscurity to center stage. As the clergy were less and less able to fulfill the increased expectations of the elder role for a whole civilization, the church found a substitute, the Mass. This vicarious authority could bring the needed sense of transcendence without the requirement of personal perfection on the part of the clergy. To be elder for the whole world was very different than being elder for just the church. The inadequacy of the old form of eldership in the context of heightened expectations left a void into which no human being could step alone. Only the shepherd, with the eucharistic symbols to point beyond oneself, could stand in that place. The tragedy of the medieval church is not that the shepherd became predominant, but that the clergy apparently neglected to examine carefully the nature of their authority and the place of the other functions.

Predominant Source of Authority

The source of authority in Medieval Christendom was confusing, as was much else. At the Council of Florence (1438-1445) the bishops received the ministry of orders. Yet prior to this many cases existed of presbyters ordaining both bishop and fellow presbyters. This kind of authority undoubtedly accrued to

51

the presbyters as a result of their greater sacerdotal responsibilities.[36] Furthermore, the cathedral canons had sole right to select their own bishop.[37] Thus the church vested authority sometimes in the hand of individuals, sometimes a group. The one constant was the total church as an ultimate, but nebulous, source of all authority.

Not only was the official position unclear, the actual practice was worse. The close, yet often antagonistic, relationship between church and state produced a turbulent disorientation. Kings, barons, lords of all kinds attempted to exercise the power of investiture, the naming of their own choice to an ecclesiastical office. Even the papacy became a victim, with anti-popes a frequent occurrence. As a result, the appointee often took orders from secular superiors as well as ecclesiastical authorities. Furthermore, the quality of the clergy decreased markedly when the motives for appointment became more political than spiritual. This period was full of unfaithful shepherds more concerned with wealth and power than with God or the needs of men and women.[38]

Consequently, the primary source of authority remained a confused tangle of "Catholic" church and powerful individual, both ecclesiastical and secular. The one bright spot was the ingenious mixture of strong authority and representative government in some of the monastic orders.[39] The general confusion was reflected in the cathedrals. Though their central location in the city, and the awesome gothic architecture did symbolize "The Church," when one entered for worship or confession she or he was likely to be greeted by the statue of a king or queen alongside the saints.[40]

The transition of primary source of authority from the individual to this state of confusion began with the demise of the eldership function. When the bishops ceased to be fully dependable authority figures, their function as sources of authority also had to decline. The initial attempt to bolster the status of the individual source of authority found expression in the growth of the papacy during the fifth century. During this time the Bishop of Rome acquired more and more influence, often because of good leadership as well as the prominence of the city.[41] However, even this development of a "chief bishop," though it represented a continuation of individual authority, removed this authority even further from the local congregation and identified it more with "The Church." Finally, the papacy itself ultimately proved unable to adequately fill the shoes of eldership. This was demonstrated by the occurrence of impropriety on the part of some medieval popes, resulting in the ascension of anti-popes. Such developments served only to confuse, and thus undermine, papal authority.

Once again, a vicarious substitute was installed. Penance, with its authorized disciplines, was the authority behind the higher clergy who heard confessions of lower clergy. It undergirded all the clergy as they issued penalties to the laity. Here, too, was the vague authority of "The Church," far above and beyond the reach of the vast majority. Thus, the same factors that propelled shepherding into prominence, also catapulted the church, in its most remote sense, into the forefront as a source of authority. Initially the church leadership attempted to share this granting of authority with the laity. Yet too much of the base had already eroded with the previous decline in power of laity and lower clergy. Thus, although penance began as a public practice, it regressed to the private confessional in the fifth and sixth centuries.[42] Another vestige of lay influence was their share in the election of a bishop and appointment of presbyters. The common people had lost most of their power centuries before the High Middle Ages. Yet, until the ninth century, the hierarchy, including bishops and secular nobles, did still bring the candidate before them to receive their assent by acclamation. However, even this practice disappeared as the feudal lords and kings of the ninth and tenth centuries challenged the faltering system.

Secular Parallels

The medieval bishops not only patterned themselves after the feudal lords and nobles, they usually functioned in that capacity. They parcelled out the church's vast territories to vassals, and were, in turn, vassals of the king.[43] As we have seen, their selection process was often the same as well. Like the secular lords, dukes, or counts, they had the responsibility of protecting their subjects, giving advice, keeping peace, and exercising guardianship over any orphan children.[44] The less scrupulous of the clergy were perfect replicas of these secular shepherds who were largely unfaithful. Absorbed in their own interests, the nobles tended to forget

53

police duty, and sometimes were a carousing menace
themselves.[45]

The ultimate twin symbols for this age were the
Holy Roman Emperor and the Pope,[46] their parallel
prominence being manifested by their rivalry for
power. Behind them also lay the latent superpowers of
"The Church" and "The Empire," beyond the reach of
common people, but influential sources of authority
nevertheless.

Another important model for church leadership
during the disease-ridden Middle Ages was the physician. The rise in the twelfth century of secular
schools for the study of medicine indicate its prominence within medieval society.[47] In the physician
the more conscientious clergy found an excellent
shepherding model of diagnosis and remedy. Corrector
Et Medicus, a pastoral manual containing corrections
for bodies and medicines for souls, revealed, by its
title alone, the medical influence on pastoral
care.[48]

Other Functions

We have already noted the disintegration of the
eldership function due to the lack of a universally
credible Christ figure. Parish priests were too
conventional, like the people themselves. Even when
they were scrupulous in their behavior, their respect
came, not from their person, but from their performance of the Mass and pronouncement of absolution. As
for the prince-bishop and the Pope, they were too
removed to fill this need. The monks and friars were
the only persons performing this function at all
satisfactorily. Often their very presence was, to the
masses, a replica of the supreme model of guidance and
protection found in the Good Shepherd or Holy Com-
forter.[49]

These monks and friars were also the only consistent examples of overseeing within the church. The
church hierarchy had taken administration away from
the local level, giving it a juridical form.[50] The
supervision of individuals was merely a safeguarding
measure, reluctantly accepted when the laity demanded
the right to minister. The official clergy frequently
offered too little too late, as with the "heretical"
Waldenses,[51] who, along with the monks and friars,
labored much more in the oversight of their people.
One could see the concern for overseeing in the gentle

supervision of St. Francis of Assisi, as well as the firm direction of Bernard of Fontanes who would not allow a novice to return home.[52] Yet, always, the purpose of oversight was enhancement of the individual's ministry of care and guidance, comfort and relief to others.[53]

The function of teaching, also largely obliterated by the dominance of shepherding, flourished among the same groups. The early Franciscans taught and preached repentance and the Kingdom of God as a corollary of their primary work, caring for the poor and outcast. The Dominicans worked to provide direction of souls as an "Order of Preachers" accompanied by teaching nunneries. The Austin canons promoted pastoral work by teaching, lecturing and writing. It is of little surprise that the primary figure in the re-emergence of scholarship was a Dominican, Thomas Aquinas, and that the initial scholastics were the monks, Anselm[54] and Abelard. Most teaching that was done during this era had to do with shepherding, as seen in the amount of theologizing on the doctrine of the sacraments. Furthermore, at the 4th Lateran Council (1215) the church hierarchy finally saw the need to place theologians in local churches to teach priests and others those things which pertain to the cure of souls.[55] Yet the presence of a sermon in the local parish was still a rarity in the first half of the thirteenth century.[56] Thus a slow revival of teaching occurred as the church began to feel more need for training in the art of caring.

Other Sources of Authority

The Scripture was the only source of authority which continued its demise while the church and individual competed for prominence. The 3rd Lateran Council (1179) demonstrated a lack of regard for Scripture when it refused to grant the Waldenses permission to preach from the Bible. The reason given was their status as "ignorant laymen." Yet this implied that authority given by the church through appropriate individual(s) far outweighed authority which came from the Scripture. In response to continued use of the Bible in the preaching of the Waldenses, as well as the Cathari, the church hierarchy reacted with rebuke, excommunication and inquisition. In some locales the fear of Scripture in "untrained" hands was so great that synods such as Toulouse (1229) denounced all translations and forbade

lay possession of Scripture, except for a few authorized portions.[57]   The bishop and the church protected their authority by claiming sole access to
interpret the third source.

Other Effects on Pastoral Authority and Lay Ministry

The neglect of the Scripture, together with
inadequate attention to eldership, teaching and
overseeing also meant further decline in charismatic
authority, ministry of the laity, and multiple
leadership.   The dominance of official authority
greatly increased during this period when the papacy,
as well as the church, gained power and status.
Standards of performance were no longer influential in
determining the validity of a cleric's authority, as
seen in the many misuses of investiture.   Ordination
had given the priest a special character,[58] whereby
one could perform the miracle of the eucharist, cure
human ills, and exercise an authority above question.
The priest was the indispensable person, set apart by
dress, work, and celibacy.   It took heretics such as
the Waldenses to perceive the dangers and refuse to
recognize the sacraments as valid if performed by an
unworthy priest.[59]

The inadequacy of the church's attention to the
ministry of the laity can also be seen in the
Waldenses who conferred ordination on all members,
thus stripping away this symbol of privilege.   With a
few exceptions, their zeal for lay ministry boldly
contrasted with that of the Catholic Church.   It was,
again, monastic groups that began to include laity in
the larger church.   The semi-monastic "third orders"
begun by Franciscans in the early thirteenth century
were, at first, for all laity, but gradually excluded
the married.[60]   The Cistercians, with their lay
brothers, were the first to return to the ancient
monastic tradition of including the laity.[61]

The common life of the monastic movement also set
a good example of strong individual authority within a
shared leadership.   Both the Dominicans and Franciscans had a cluster of fellow monks, called the General
Chapter, with whom the Master General governed.[62]
Outside the monastic movement, the diocesan bishop did
have a college of canons advising and assisting in the
administration, much as the Pope had his cardinals.
However, the local parish seldom felt any benefit from
this collegiality.   The parish priest, usually from
peasant stock,[63] was all too often an uneducated,

manipulated, isolated and lonely confessor. Both local priest and secular persons were dominated by the same mixture of ecclesiastical/secular powers that controlled everything. The art of caring had become more often the art of intrigue.

Conclusions

The one bright light that marks this era off from the Dark Ages was the reforms of the monastic movement. The monks and friars were largely what the church needed. They provided the respected figurehead in an age hungry for credible authorities. Their calling was charismatic in an age of officialdom. Finally, they revived teaching and demonstrated the benefits of close oversight of individuals. Yet, when many of them became powerful to the point of papal ascendance, they frequently compromised their original ideals, as with the Dominicans' involvement in the Inquisition.[64] Perhaps they were unable to resist the corrupting pressures of church hierarchy because of their natural lack of contact with the local parish. Certainly a stronger regard for the place of lay ministry, the lack of which was one of the cardinal sins of the age, would have helped. Finally, for some, a better understanding of the authority of Scripture would have given them greater direction for their enormous energy.

The Reformation

Basic Need

Martin Luther's 95 theses marked the beginning of a new era that would alter the rest of Christian history. This transition period (ca. 1517-1648) was a time of even more rapid change than the eleventh century. Discovery of new worlds and scientific experimentation had opened previously unimaginable doors. The invention of the printing press had brought increased literacy and learning. The development of secular humanism had led to a questioning of old dogmas. This uncertainty, together with the breakdown of feudalism, rise of the middle class, expansion of trade and economy, and development of individualism and nationalism, had greatly deprived the Catholic Church of power and prestige.[65] It was an exploding, exploring, investigating age that needed a church which would participate creatively in the new searching. Thus, the basic need was to learn, to broaden one's horizons, to experiment, to find a personal sense of fulfillment, to redevelop values, and to redefine faith and church life to include all that was new.

Predominant Function

These needs led naturally to the predominance of teaching as a pastoral function. Notwithstanding the diversity of Reformation groups, this focus prevailed, particularly in the preaching of the Word. Luther, in his Ordering of Worship, placed preaching in the central position, as did the government of Zurich under the leadership of Zwingli. Luther's catechisms[66] and Calvin's Instruction In Faith, written for the laity, pointed to the stress they laid on teaching. Calvinism even referred to pastors as "teaching elders." The Marian Injunctions (1554) of the Church of England required the bishop to give a homily in each parish for the instruction of the people in the Word of God. Adequate education of clergy was another universal concern, with seminaries and universities emerging throughout early Protestantism.

This new focus was even developing in the Catholic Church, a process accelerated, but not begun, by the Reformation. The Council of Trent (1545-1563) required a sermon as part of the worship in every cathedral or bishop's church. The Jesuits and Capuchins began primarily as teaching and preaching orders, respectively. In the seventeenth century, when Protestantism entered the age of scholasticism, French Catholicism became well-known for its preaching.

By this time the pastor was usually an educated person whose task was to preach and teach a systematic theology to a literate people.[67] The symbols of this time period spoke loudly of the teaching focus. The actions of Zwingli and the government of Zurich, in banishing all images, relics and organs from the churches were not uncommon.[68] The pulpit became the central feature of the Protestant place of worship.[69] Furthermore, by the end of the sixteenth century, the Anglican priest worked primarily out of a study added on to his house, another symbolic indication of the predominance of teaching.

The transition from shepherding to teaching took place primarily during the Reformation period and was essentially complete by the end of the Council of Trent. Yet it did begin prior to the Reformation as seen by the influence of Wycliffe, Huss, Occam and others on the later reformers. Two factors created the changed atmosphere of the early sixteenth century and made it possible for teaching to emerge as predominant. First, the still powerful Catholic Church was at a very low ebb morally and, hence, was a steady source of disenchantment to the growing middle class. Second, the Renaissance had revitalized both religious and secular learning, providing the possibility for new understandings of faith and church. Thus the sacramental system, with its dependence on priests, became less essential than during earlier times.[70]

Predominant Source of Authority

With the ascendance of teaching as the focal function came the predominance of Scripture as a source of authority. The primacy of "The Word" from God was a natural prerequisite for concluding the centrality of teaching what God had spoken. Yet, the needs of the age were the main reason for the rise of scriptural authority. With the past dominance of "The Church" and powerful individuals within it, the Scriptures represented the only feasible alternative for a world looking to experiment and broaden its horizons. Furthermore, it lent itself uniquely to the needs for learning, developing new values, and redefining both church and faith. In contrast to the church or an individual, one could study it and gain fresh ideas and perspectives. But, most important for this age of growing individualism, it presented the opportunity to discover one's own "individual" interpretation and understanding plus find one's own "personal" sense of fulfillment.

Prior to Luther the Scriptures were already a growing focus for study. Luther owed much to humanists like Erasmus who first opened his eyes to the possibilities of literal study and re-interpretation of the Bible.[71] Zwingli credited his humanistic instructor, Thomas Wyttenback, with teaching him the sole authority of Scripture. Though we can find some pre-Reformation examples of high regard for Scripture, its near universal predominance was unique. Luther considered it important enough to translate into the German tongue. Plus, when asked about the format of worship, he asserted the need to keep the Word of God central. The Anabaptist, Hubmaier, declared the Bible to be the sole law of the church, while Marpeck justified Anabaptist doctrine on the basis of strict Biblicism.

Calvin developed the most thorough statement of the authority of Scripture. To him the Bible was the voice of God which both church and society must use as guide for any structuring of authority. Thus it became the basis for governmental forms, as well as the process of leadership selection, in both Genevan society and the Reformed Church. Everything the ruler did, and everything the pastor preached, had to be in accord with the Scripture.

In the Roman Catholic Church it is questionable whether Scripture ever became the primary source of authority. The Council of Trent proclaimed the church as the final authority. Yet the very fact that it dealt at great length with the Scripture issue, plus granted it equal status with tradition and required its public interpretation in the larger towns, demonstrated an increased significance within the Catholic Church.[72] In the Church of England, where the Reformation also did not completely prevail, the priests were still expected to be expositors of the Word.[73] As a challenge to former conceptions, the Scripture's full acceptance on the part of those whom it challenged would have been unlikely. Yet their solid appropriation of it signified its unusual importance.

On the other hand, one can see its degree of influence within Protestantism by, again, noting the removal of all images, relics and organs from the church buildings of Zwingli's Zurich. The pulpit with the open Bible was the central feature of Protestantism. These Scriptures were at the core of worship, study, and all aspects of church life and leadership.

Secular Parallels

We have already noted the increase of learning, literacy, and scientific experimentation during this age. When we further observe that Luther, Zwingli and Calvin were all scholars, the latter two originally humanistic,[74] it becomes clear that the scholar was the model for the new church leadership role with its teaching focus. The scholar-professor was increasing rapidly in prestige just prior to the Reformation. In Germany alone, fourteen universities were founded between 1386 and 1506. Many modern disciplines trace their beginnings to the time of Da Vinci (1452-1519), Machiavelli (1469-1527) and Copernicus (1473-1543).

The humanism which inspired these and others grew out of a respect for the ancient Greek and Roman classics. Some of the Italian humanists were so insistent on the superior nature of the works of antiquity that they would use only the limiting vocabulary and style of an ancient writer, rejecting both the Italian language and the "corrupted" Latin used in the church. Moreover, they tried to dress, talk, and behave as an ancient Roman. In sort, they used the ancient classics as a written source of authority in much the same way the reformers used the Scriptures. They both shared the same excitement over getting back to the original, brushing aside the corruption induced by the Middle Ages. Each had their liberalists who would insist on absolute purity of form, be it literature or theological doctrine. Each had the naive extremist who would only act according to the exact letter of the ancient writings, attempting to live in antiquity itself.

Later, humanism developed most particularly in the direction of rapid scientific advancement, with the likes of Vesalius (1514-1564), Bacon (1561-1626), Galileo (1564-1642), Kepler (1571-1630) and Descartes (1596-1650). By the middle of the seventeenth century, the scientific view had become the "new knowledge" accepted all over Europe.[75] The Church, continuing to take its lead from the scholars, again entered an age of scholasticism, developing and imparting its own brand of knowledge. This whole age had become reconstituted around reason and the written word, so also did the church and its leadership.[76]

Other Functions

The other functions of the pastoral role all appeared during the Reformation, each one being formed according to the needs of the times. The pastor filled the role of elder as the respected, learned person. This "man of Letters" was often the best educated of the congregation. In the seventeenth century the term "parson" became a popular designation for the pastor. Coming from the Latin, "persona," this terminology indicated that the pastor was "the person" of the parish. However, from the disrepute into which this term fell, we must conclude that the

61

pastor was not performing this function satisfactorily at the end of the Reformation period.[77]

In the shepherding of individuals the Reformation pastor departed greatly from medieval practices. Though different views on the Lord's Supper existed, Protestants did not see the pastor as the primary source of one's relationship with God. That relationship was a matter of faith. Therefore the shepherding centered more around guidance in doctrinal purity, rather than imparting of God's grace through the performance of the eucharist. Church discipline also changed, from the private issuance of a salvific penalty through the sacrament of penance, to a way of publicly enforcing doctrinal and moral purity within the Lutheran and Reformed communions. The strong connection between shepherding and teaching lasted into the seventeenth century when the purpose of a house call was to speak about the spiritual condition of everyone in the home. The pastor usually delivered an actual sermon. Never did one make a mere social visit, as that would have violated the serious nature of the task.[78]

The same tendency appeared in the overseeing function. One clear example was Luther's attempt to organize the country parishes. He sent out "theologians" and "lawyers" equipped with copies of his catechisms, a German Bible, and his own sermons which he expected his emissaries to memorize and deliver.[79] One wonders how much they "looked over" or "overheard" while preaching and exhorting. Everywhere, emphasis was on pure doctrine and its resulting moral life. Thus we can conclude that all three remaining functions did exist, but each one somewhat truncated by the fascination of the age, teaching.

Other Sources of Authority

The church and the individual, as sources of authority, both appeared in the Reformation churches, though not in any universally consistent pattern. Each group interpreted the primary source of authority, Scripture, in a different way, thus developing a multitude of attitudes toward the church and individual as sources of authority.

Luther, at first, allowed each congregation the power to appoint and depose its pastor. However, his opinion changed as a result of the expanse of territory under his influence, his distrust of the common person after the Peasant's War, and the desire for control on the part of Elector John of Saxony. The final form of church government provided for a super-intendent who had spiritual, but not administrative, authority over the parish minister, and who, in turn, was subject to the Elector of the state. Thus the individual became more powerful than the church in early Lutheranism.

Calvin gave more power to the church people, allowing them a voice in choosing their officers. In actual practice this control was exercised by the city council of theocratic Geneva, a group very much influenced by Calvin himself. However, later, Calvin did separate church and state, giving the church the decisive hand in granting authority.

The Anabaptists are the hardest to categorize. They usually verbalized little respect for any authority other than Scripture. In practice they depended on the leading of the Spirit, as when the original founders of the movement were rebaptized. During a prayer meeting one of them asked another to assume the authority to baptize him, after which he, himself, assumed the authority to baptize the rest.[80] In this case it was the individual in whom authority was vested. Yet it became recognized only in the community's discernment of the leading of the Spirit.

Other Effects on Pastoral Authority and Lay Ministry

The Reformation period reversed many trends which had been developing for over a thousand years. Though it is difficult to generalize this era's conceptions of ministry of the laity, basis of authority, and recipients of authority, patterns did exist. Re-emergence of the doctrine of the priesthood of all believers, affirmed by all the reformers, resulted in greater stress on the ministry of the laity. Calvin demonstrated this by his inclusion of lay people on the Consistoire, the governing council.[81] Despite this good start, however, Reformation churches did not maintain this emphasis beyond the early decades of the sixteenth century.[82] Secondly, Calvin developed one of the best balances between multiple and singleheaded leadership in Christian history. The clergy did have direct control over preaching and teaching. Yet the Consistoire, including numbers of laymen, was responsible for governing the church.[83] Finally, official authority no longer dominated the church.

The Protestant clergy did not possess special sacramental powers. They were ordained to perform a function, not to be part of an order.[84] Thus, one could challenge their authority and question their fitness on the basis of poor performance. This was a major change from Catholicism, a very significant reassertion of the validity of charismatic authority. Some groups in the Reformation, overreacting against Catholicism, overemphasized charismatic authority as well as the plurality of leadership. This was understandable considering the degree of imbalance they initially faced. Yet such extreme reactions were not constructive in the long run.

Conclusions

In summary, the Reformation pastorate was, by and large, fairly healthy. Yet, if church leaders had placed more emphasis on developing the unique place of the non-teaching functions, they might have avoided the decline of lay ministry. Sensitive shepherding and overseeing would certainly have assisted in the development of strong, motivated, lay leadership. Secondly, some sectarian groups, as just mentioned, would have done well to regain a sense of official authority. The leadership of the church would then have had a stronger foundation from which to equip the saints for the work of ministry and the building up of the body of Christ.

1. H. Richard Niebuhr, The Purpose of the Church and Its Ministry: Reflection On The Aims of Theological Education (New York: Harper & Brothers, 1956), pp. 80-81.

2. Williston Walker, A History of the Christian Church, revised by Cyril Richardson, Wilhelm Pauck and Robert Handy (New York: Charles Scribner's Sons, 1959), pp. 78-81.

3. Urban T. Holmes III, The Future Shape of Ministry: A Theological Projection (New York: The Seabury Press, 1971), pp. 26-31.

4. J. W. C. Wand, A History of the Early Church to A.D. 500 (4th ed.; Norwich, Great Britain: Jarrold and Sons Ltd., 1963), pp. 91-92.

5. Walker, p. 23.

6. Wand, p. 118.

7. Walker, p. 83.

8. Wand, p. 92.

9. Walker, pp. 59-60.

10. Hans Kung, The Church, trans. by Ray and Rosaleen Ockenden (New York: Sheed and Ward, 1967), p. 412.

11. Tape by Ben Johnson, Foundations For The Emerging Church: Contemporary Expression, Session 4 (Waco, Texas: Word Publications, 1971).

12. Walker, p. 82.

13. Wallace K. Ferguson A Survey of European Civilization Part One to 1660, ed. by William L. Langer (3rd. ed., Boston: Houghton Mifflin Co., 1962), pp. 79-80.

14.   William A. Clebsch and Charles R. Jaekle, _Pastoral Care In Historical Perspective_ (Englewood Cliffs, N. J.: Prentice-Hall, Inc., 1964), pp. 17-19.

15.   Holmes, p. 32.

16.   _Ibid_.

17.   Walker, pp. 58-60.

18.   Holmes, p. 32.

19.   Wand, p. 110.

20.   Holmes, p. 55.

21.   Wand, pp. 119-120.

22.   Holmes, pp. 30-31.

23.   _Ibid_., p. 26.

24.   Wand, pp. 111, 120-122.

25.   Kung, _The Church_, p. 412.

26.   Clebsch and Jaekle, p. 13.

27.   _Ibid_., p. 24.

28.   Robert Brow, _Religion And Ideas_ (Chicago: Inter-Varsity Press, 1966), p. 26.

29.   John T. McNeill, _A History of the Cure of Souls_ (New York: Harper and Brother Publishers, 1951), pp. 109, 119, 146, 149, 160.

30.   Clebsch and Jaekle, pp. 24, 34-35.

31.   Holmes, p. 52.

32.   McNeill, p. 148.

33.   Ferguson, pp. 239, 268-270.

34.   McNeill, pp. 109-110.

35.   Holmes, pp. 34-36.

36.   _Ibid_., p. 55.

37. Ferguson, p. 253.

38. _Ibid._, pp. 167-168.

39. Walker, p. 233.

40. Ferguson, pp. 253-254.

41. Walker, pp. 123-124.

42. Holmes, pp. 43-44.

43. Ferguson, pp. 167-168.

44. American R. D. M. Corporation, _A Study Out-line For World History_ (New York: American R. D. M. Corporation, 1962), p. 40.

45. Ferguson, pp. 223-224.

46. Clebsch and Jaekle, p. 24.

47. Margaret Deanesly, _A History of the Medieval Church 590-1500_ (8th ed.; London: Unwin Brothers Limited, 1954), p. 134.

48. Clebsch and Jaekle, p. 24.

49. Holmes, pp. 47-48.

50. _Ibid._, p. 56.

51. Walker, p. 230.

52. Deanesly, p. 121.

53. Walker, pp. 232-235.

54. _Ibid._, pp. 230-235, 239, 245.

55. Deanesly, pp. 138, 152.

56. Holmes, p. 51.

57. Walker, pp. 229-231.

58. Holmes, p. 56.

59. Walker, p. 230.

60. <u>Ibid</u>., pp. 230, 236-237.

61. Deanesley, pp. 122-123.

62. Walker, pp. 233-237.

63. Ferguson, p. 253.

64. Walker, p. 232.

65. Holmes, pp. 58-60.

66. Walker, pp. 314, 319, 323.

67. Holmes, pp. 62-72.

68. Walker, p. 323.

69. Niebuhr, pp. 60, 80.

70. Ferguson, pp. 374-376.

71. <u>Ibid</u>., p. 376.

72. Walker, pp. 311-314, 322-330, 349-352, 378.

73. Holmes, p. 66

74. Walker, pp. 303, 321-322, 349.

75. R. R. Palmer, <u>A History of the Modern World</u>, revised with the collaboration of Joel Colton (2nd. ed.; New York: Alfred A. Knopf, Inc., 1956), pp. 52-57, 261-269.

76. Holmes, p. 95.

77. <u>Ibid</u>., pp. 69, 74.

78. <u>Ibid</u>., pp. 62-63, 72.

79. <u>Ibid</u>., p. 62.

80. Walker, pp. 314, 319, 326, 352.

81. <u>Ibid</u>., p. 354.

82. Holmes, p. 60.

83. Walker, p. 354.

84. Holmes, p. 61.

PART II

A CONTEMPORARY PERSPECTIVE

CHAPTER IV

AN INITIAL SKETCH

Contemporary images of role and authority must be based on Scripture and informed by history. Some details in this initial sketch come directly from the Scriptures. Any new images must certainly include the three sources of authority, the four functions, and a balance of both single-multiple leadership styles and charismatic-official authority. In addition, the understanding of ministry must be broad enough, not only to include the laity, but to encourage them in service to Christ. Then, as in other periods of history, the basic need of our time must determine both predominant function and source of authority. In each case, there will be parallels in secular society, as well as symbolic indications of their emergence within the life of the church and the work of the church leader. In addition it will be important to indicate the way in which each remaining function and source of authority can help fill the basic need. Finally, one must investigate potential pitfalls, through comparison with past history, prior to examining each of the functions in succeeding chapters. However, before beginning, it will be helpful to describe the transition period from which we are just now emerging.

Stage Of Transition

The twentieth century has been another time in history when enormous change has taken place in all aspects of life. Unprecedented gains in science and technology have sent us from horse and buggy to the moon. Yet along with this "progress" has come greater alienation. Sophisticated technology has brought bigger and more destructive wars. Due to greater mobility, people no longer live all their lives in one community near grandparents, aunts and uncles. Communities and neighborhoods are more impersonal, bureaucratic, and cold. Society is increasingly heterogeneous. Yet primary group relationships usually consist of like-minded individuals. Young and old often have less interaction, seemingly less in common. Furthermore, trusted institutions and customs have declined. Old authority structures have broken down. In the midst of all this, first suburbia, and then gentrification, has offered escape from decay and

73

crime. Television and other diversions have offered escape from family, neighbors, and social organizations, including the church.

The initial response of the church to this breakdown of relationships was the baptism of individuality. Each person had his own understanding of the faith, her own private relationship with God. Each church had its own closed, and often declining, constituency. Each pastor had one's own conception of the role, and determined one's own source of authority to justify it. For many people, the teaching emphasis of the Reformation was still the focal point of church life despite its tattered state as seen in the decline of the Sunday school. Piety and doctrine remained their primary concerns. Others took up the banners of pastoral care and social involvement. This individualistic approach to all of church life was largely responsible for the state of confusion that still exists to some degree today in leadership role and authority.

Emerging Foci

As a society of isolated, and often lonely, individuals, we need a sense of community where each person has a significant place and part. We need to be participants with others in something meaningful in order to give us a sense of belonging, of being a part of a people. In a society which does not provide this community life it is of utmost importance that the church become this community for its members, as well as those outside to whom God calls it to minister.

To emphasize building the community is also to say that "body of Christ", "fellowship of the Spirit," and "new creation," are the primary images of today's church. Certainly any examination of current church literature will find it heavily weighted in favor of these symbols. Body of Christ, as with fellowship of the Spirit, is an image which requires the participation of everyone. Each member is important to the functioning of the whole. Thus committed lay involvement is equally as important as the dedication of the clergy. Moreover, the predominant function and source of authority should be those which best facilitate this ministry of the laity.

In this light, the predominant source of authority clearly becomes the church, the community that is

74

the body of Christ. The church is the only source that, by its very nature, gives the laity a part in the granting of authority. This step is terribly important if the laity are to become full participants in the body. For one needs to give a person or group a share in the source of power before one can ever expect their meaningful participation. Furthermore, if one wishes to secure total participation at a time when expectations for meaningful community are low, then it will be necessary to give laity the primary share in the granting of authority. Secondly, by much the same reasoning, overseeing must become the predominant function today. If the primary image of the church is the body of Christ, then the focal point of leadership function is to encourage the use of individual gifts, ensure their proper exercise, and guide the expression of them toward the unity and edification of the whole church. In short, the church leader's prime concern must be the care, or oversight, of the church. This function alone necessitates the active involvement of the laity. Sheep can merely follow the clear path laid out for them by the shepherd. Pupils can merely sit quietly and listen to the teacher. The "younger" can merely lie at the feet of the elder, soaking up all the wisdom. But one whom the pastor oversees, must actively perform a task of some kind.

Modern church architecture illustrates these emerging foci of overseer and church authority. H. Richard Niebuhr speaks of the modern church building, with its multi-purpose rooms, as an indication of the predominance of the overseer, or pastoral director as he calls him. Even the pews in the place of worship are often movable, making the room functional for a variety of purposes. The pastor no longer works out of a study, reminiscent of the old teaching focus. Instead there is a church office from which one can oversee the ministry of the church.[1] These symbols of multi-functional use and director's office imply the presence of much activity on the part of persons other than the pastor. Therefore, in addition to symbolizing the predominance of overseeing, the signs also demonstrate that the "ecclesia", the gathered body of Christ, is the primary source of authority.

Concern over issues of oversight and management have recently been the subject of much study in the church. Yet one can also see the emergence of this overseeing role outside the church. As seen by the titles of our secular leadership today, our society perceives them primarily as overseers. Business has its managers, education its superintendents, and government its executives. Hospital administrators, baseball managers, theater directors and prison superintendents are among many other examples. Furthermore, the nature of secular overseeing today is greatly altered from past generations. The good business manager is not one who lords it over subordinates. Instead, one recognizes that the whole organization has the ultimate power to make or break the enterprise. The real source of authority must come from the entire group. Recognizing this is not only a key to successful business management, but also effective church administration. A detailed examination of this will be the subject of the next chapter. For now, it is sufficient to conclude that a parallel also exists between secular and religious sources of authority.

Completing The Outline

The remaining functions and sources of authority must now be integrated into the developing model. Each must be incorporated in such a way that it serves that basic need which determines the predominant foci. First, Scripture as a source of authority is subordinate to its primary interpreter, the church. Thus its collective interpretation is more significant for a situation than simply the Scripture itself or its private interpretation by individuals. Nonetheless, these Scriptures do provide revelation from God concerning divine purposes for, not only individuals, but even more, the church. Without a high regard for the Scriptures, a church could easily cease to function as a vehicle for communicating the gospel. The body of Christ is in danger of malfunction when it ignores the only objective revelation of its Head, and the only external, authoritative guide against which it can test and check itself. Moreover, the Scripture is our link with the origins of community life in the church. It comes not only from God, but from the apostolic community as well. Its authors are part of our larger community, sharing with us in written form. They are our roots. Understanding where we come from is always an important element in any realization of who we are and what we are to be about.

The presence of an individual source of authority in the person of bishop, district superintendent, area minister, etc., keeps both local pastor and congregation from losing a sense of the official basis of their authority. This individual source is visible, tangible and official in nature. Without it the local church community may cease to relate effectively to the wider church, or even to function in an orderly and decisive manner itself. Frequently, the voice of the community lacks clarity. Often the Scripture lacks specificity for contemporary situations. Hence the clear, specific guidance of the individual is indispensable. When the church leader does use the individual as a source of authority, one must see that person as a representative of the church, both past and present. As a representative of the past church, this individual, who is the source of authority, personifies the sacred tradition. Apostolic succession is one attempt to justify viewing the individual as a representative of tradition, a source of authority. However, church leaders from differing communions will still need to understand these individuals in this manner. As a representative of the present church, this individual, who is the source of authority, symbolizes the whole church. Again, the high church tradition already advocates this perspective, though the temptation does exist to forget that the individual is primarily a symbol. In the low church tradition, which supposes local autonomy, church leaders must learn to utilize their area and conference ministers, senior pastors, et al., but in ways that still respect the local congregation as the primary source of authority. In chapter 8, I will further develop the implications of all three sources along with other issues of pastoral authority.

The three remaining functions not only serve to fulfill the basic need, they are also the foundation that supports the primary function of overseeing. We can conceive of the interplay between the various functions in much the same way as in Maslow's concept of the hierarchy of needs in personality theory. According to this theory individuals' needs arrange themselves in a hierarchy from most basic, such as food and safety, to higher-level, such as self-esteem and actualization. Unless one satisfies the basic needs, their lack of fulfillment will dominate one's behavior. However, if one gratifies these basic needs, then one will be free to fulfill the higher-level ones upon which rest the attainment of full potential as a human being. Thus, only through satisfaction of lower-level needs, can higher-level

ones become dominant without jeopardizing or stultify-
ing the development of one's potential.[2]

Likewise the church leader, before exercising
effective oversight, must first teach people how to
minister in the name of Christ. Second, before the
laity will open themselves up to be taught, the church
leader will need to become the shepherd who cares.
Finally, before they are willing to entrust anyone
with their needs and hurts, the church leader will
have to be an effective elder or authority figure.
Each level is essential to the next, beginning with
eldership, the foundation of leadership function.
Thus there may be times in the life of a given church
when severe deficiencies in one of the lower-levels
necessitates giving most of one's attention to a
function other than overseeing. Yet we must never
lose sight of that toward which, and for which, we are
building. The church will not fulfill its potential
as the needed community, the body of Christ, until the
higher-level needs of the church are met.

In this light the purpose of eldership is to
personify the communal authority which undergirds the
very life of the body of Christ. The elder represents
all the traditions which hold this community together.
Only with the vitality of this living tradition, embodied in the elder, can individuals find the courage
to continue risking themselves in ministry to both one
another and the world.

The initial task of shepherding will be to heal
the hurts of lonely, isolated people and reconcile
those whose differences are affecting the unity and
ministry of the church. Secondly, the shepherd must
help guide persons into particular ministries consistent with their gifts and give support to groups and
individuals performing these ministries. Persons at
all stages of involvement and ministry are going to
need the open ears and warm hearts of understanding
shepherds. Furthermore, their ministries will be most
effective if the people with whom they work can also
turn to a shepherd. Many times the lay person may be
able to act as an undershepherd. Yet the pastor must
also be available to such persons outside the church.

The primary focus of teaching becomes the training and instruction needed to prepare and enable men
and women to minister to others in the name of Christ.
It is the process of equipping the saints for the work
of ministry and the building up of the body of Christ.

The teacher will become the facilitator, stimulator, and resource person of the community for the sake of its unity and mission. Thus the content of teaching and preaching will emphasize both the learning of ministry skills and the building of character into mature personhood, into "the measure of the stature of the fullness of Christ." If this teaching is successful, a church will begin to discover the emergence of para-professional laity who can, by word and deed, interpret to others the meaning of Christian faith.

Since these remaining functions are essential to the effectiveness of the church leader, the neglect of any one could thwart the growth of the whole church body. In the past, history has shown us the tendency for the predominant function to overshadow, and in some cases nearly eliminate, the others. This same danger exists today and could be fatal to the life of the church.

Avoiding Past Mistakes

The overshadowing of non-predominant functions has been the result of various causes during different periods of history. Each period serves as a warning of similar pitfalls today. The third century church confused the functions of elder and overseer by the title they chose. We also must take care not to confuse ourselves by frequently describing the pastoral role with such titles as "preacher" which reflect the previous days of the teaching focus. Important as preaching is, it is no longer the integrating title that it once was. On the other hand, the church of the Middle Ages never recovered from the transition period centuries earlier, when the shepherding function rushed in to fill the void left by the decline of eldership. We must be extremely careful at this point, for we, as in the fourth century, have been without any predominant focus. If we were to allow overseeing to so capture our imagination that nothing else mattered, the results could be just as devastating today as they were in the High Middle Ages. One precautionary step, which the earlier church neglected, is to be aware that we are adopting a particular predominant function, and conscious of the danger involved. However, church leaders during the Reformation were very aware that they were proposing something new. Although this period was one of the brightest in church history, they still were not able to curb the overshadowing effect of the predominant function. Thus, anyone who urges the adoption of one particular focus must still take extreme care to develop the subordinate functions.

The same may be said of the need for balance among the sources of authority. Again history shows us the dangers. In the third century, the church had become so comfortable with the individual as a source of authority that it let the scriptural tradition, which had once been predominant, almost slip away unnoticed. It is very natural to neglect a formerly predominant source of authority that appears to have proved inadequate to changing times and needs. In our day, the Scriptures, again the "old" predominant source of authority, have undergone a period of severe questioning. Biblical criticism has eroded the old understandings, leaving it rather ill-defined as an authority source. While we are formulating new conceptions, we will need to take great care not to become so comfortable with our communal source that we neglect the Scriptures. The same warning also applies to the individual source. As a result of the individualistic period, out of which we have just emerged, our tendency is to suspect anything which gives one individual too much power. However, the community cannot fill all of our need for an authority source. To wait for this impossibility would be like the church leaders of the Middle Ages waiting for their vicarious authority source, penance, to fill the need. Some hope can be taken from the Catholic Church after the Reformation. They seemed to weather well the transition to the predominance of a scriptural authority source. This change was not of their choosing, undoubtedly not of their liking. Yet they learned from it, to the benefit of the whole church. So too, present day reformers may bend us in ways we do not like, in directions which go against the grain of our traditions and preconceptions. If we can be open to these new winds of the Spirit, we might find that this Wind has blown us into a far more productive place than we could have imagined.

From Sketch To Final Picture

The next step is to discover the precise understanding needed in order for each function and source of authority to do its part in meeting the basic need for community. Consequently, each function will be examined separately in the next four chapters, before concluding with the final picture. In each case a secular profession, and the way it attempts to meet the need for community, will become a model for church leadership role. Since all issues relating to authority, including its source, are basic to that bedrock upon which the other leadership functions are built, all further discussion of this will be included in the one chapter on that subject. Finally, the starting point will be the highest level, the point of greatest potential fulfillment, namely, the function of overseeing which builds toward the ministry of the laity. Hopefully, we will better understand the function of each lower-level if we first examine the layer toward which it builds.

NOTES

1. H. Richard Niebuhr, <u>The Purpose of The Church and Its Ministry: Reflections On The Aims of Theological Education</u> (New York: Harper & Brothers, 1956), pp. 80-81.

2. Abraham H. Maslow, <u>Motivation and Personality</u> (2nd ed.; New York: Harper and Row, 1970), pp. 97-100.

CHAPTER   V

ADMINISTRATION

Many secular occupations are available as models
for the central function of overseeing.   It has already been demonstrated that management has become a
leading institution in our society.   Yet when one
thinks of an executive, manager, or administrator, the
first image that comes to mind is that of the business
world.   Administration is an integral part of business, which has consequently done much to develop the
art of management.   Thus, it is natural to draw upon
this model to inform an understanding of the present-
day church overseer or administrator.   The specific
model I will use represents a very recent trend in the
field, one that arose in response to our basic need
for community.   Robert Blake and Jane Mouton describe
a process for charting one's managerial style in their
book, The Managerial Grid.   They list two commonly
accepted postulates in any management theory, concern
for production and concern for people.   They propose
that the most effective managerial style is one which
includes maximum concern for both people and production, a style they call 9,9 management.[1]

9,9 Managerial Style

The key to 9,9 managerial style is the relationship of common understanding and vision which develops
between manager and subordinates.   This style of management emphasizes participation on the part of each
person in the process of setting, implementing and
evaluating all proposals.   In 9,9 managerial style,
the attempt is to fit the organization to the individual, not vice versa, yet without ignoring the need for
production.[2]   However, some sense of community is
basic to the effectiveness of anything an organization
decides to do.   There should be a sense of shared
responsibility.   No one should be able to say, "I am
totally responsible for this; you are totally responsible for that."[3]

The creativity of each individual is important in
furthering the growth capacity of the firm.   However,
a degree of conformity is necessary for any sense of
cohesion or joint effort.   The organization, rather
than the individual, must become the primary unit of

83

development, making organizational development more important than management training.[4]

Fundamental to this process is the understanding that the manager, alone, does not direct the task. Instead, he or she works to establish direction by employing various problem solving strategies in relation to the major work units of the organization.[5] To adequately understand this model, it will be helpful to first examine the various work units which 9,9 management utilizes and then investigate the basic responsibilities common to the manager's role within each unit.

Major Work Units

In 9,9 managerial style, the major work units, in addition to the whole organization, are teams, supervisor-subordinate pairs, and individuals. Business organizations need good team performance, good solo effort, and good pair action. Development and supervision of each work unit is necessary. Yet development of the team is most critical. The manager can say many things once to the whole team rather than repeat them to each individual or working pair. This development of team action should begin with the top level team in any given organization, because they have the most influence and can set an example for others.[6]

The manager's relationship to each major work unit constitutes a unique problem solving strategy. Consequently, common strategies include: one person working alone, two persons working together (pair action), a whole team working together, and an entire organization working together. The more inclusive and significant the problem, the greater the need to involve everyone. Yet other factors may also influence the choice of strategy. When time is unavailable for discussion, the manager should not include everyone. Likewise, when needed information is in the hands of one or two individuals, then it is a waste of time to include the rest. However, if several people need to be involved in the pooling of information, then, of course, all should participate.[7]

Manager Development

Even though the focus of 9,9 management training is on the team and organization, the process starts with the development of the individual manager in a

Lab Seminar Training program. In this program the manager must study the grid concepts prior to attendance. Second, there is evaluation of one's own managerial style by completing various tests. Third, one is assigned to a team, which is given problem-solving exercises in order to evaluate their own behavior and problem-solving capability. This includes giving feedback to individuals by other members regarding managerial style.[8] In this way the manager can learn much about how he or she functions as an individual, as a part of a supervisor-subordinate pair, as a team member, and as a member of the organization.

Pair Action Development

A good supervisory relationship between manager and subordinates is necessary for a healthy organization. Such a relationship requires openness and candid exchange as well as the active participation of both supervisor and subordinate in any decision-making, implementation, or evaluation. The manager does not assign the tasks. Instead they grow out of mutually accepted goals and objectives. Performance evaluation also relates to these goals and objectives. Periodically, the supervisor and supervisee need to write evaluations of each other to discern any progress.[9]

Team Development

Teams consist of a manager and all of her or his subordinates. Each individual, with the exception of top manager and front line worker, is a part of two teams. On one team, the person is the manager and on the other a subordinate. Each of these teams develops its own culture, style of interaction, manner of accomplishing routine operations, etc. The growth of these teams rests on the ability to freeze the process at some point in order to evaluate various cultural barriers to team effectiveness and to plan ahead. In teamwork development the attempt is to analyze, study and correct procedures. Each individual should be able to see how well he or she performs, how well they as a team coordinate efforts, how well they take advantage of unforeseen opportunities, and how high or low is the team spirit.[10]

Organizational Development

Organizational development involves designing the structure of the organization and working out the relationships between its various groups. All levels must have input into the process of designing or redesigning. The final outcome should be a structure in which communication is smooth, natural, and all-inclusive, with a headquarters organization which can best provide a capacity for generating investment and developing talent.[11] Once the structure is set, there will still be difficulties in relationship between various work groups. The company must first find a means to bring to light these operating tensions. Then group members, and/or their representatives, must talk these through with one another. The object is to move from having winners and losers to having one united effort to solve the problem.[12]

Managerial Responsibilities

There are three major managerial responsibilities in 9,9 management. The manager must see that planning, work execution, and follow-up are effectively accomplished.

Planning

According to Peter Drucker, strategic planning, either long or short range, is the process of systematically making risky decisions with as much knowledge of future effects as possible. In the broadest sense it includes organizing the implementation or execution of the work and designing the evaluation or follow-up.[13] The 9,9 manager, who is responsible for seeing that good planning occurs, should utilize those who have the relevant facts, as well as those with a stake in the outcome. Together, they need to proceed toward clear and realistic goals by identifying the key problem, analyzing it, developing alternative solutions, and deciding on the best course of action. Finally, the manager needs to assign each person a particular responsibility for implementation of the solution and set out the sequence of steps required.[14]

Any strategic planning must take place on a higher level than manager development. The whole team or organization should be the central planning unit. To

86

adequately develop organizational goals, one must in-clude a cross section of the whole company. This "diagonal slice" of the organization is better equipped than any other one group to find out the problems that exist between departments and which affect the whole organization.[15]

Throughout the process, the planning group, at any level, must select projects on the basis of the interests and abilities of the personnel, keeping in mind the need for the whole community to "own" any given endeavor. In addition, it is usually possible, and important, to provide for each person a unique and challenging role. Finally, those involved in the planning must ensure that each individual's contribu-tion is a complete step in the process.[16]

Work Execution

When the organization does implement this plan, the manager needs to help people see the implications, particularly for themselves, and gain the confidence and ability to perform the task. To attain a particu-lar organizational goal within the ideal model, the manager has to gain the participation of the various teams and provide them with necessary information. Then, together, they should discuss the nature of the problem and proceed to take corrective steps.[17]

The manager is in a unique position, independent of the rest of the group or team, to prevent and/or remove obstacles which block a worker's motivation to work toward an agreed upon goal. Moreover, he or she is in the best position to moderate any conflict which emerges during the proposed venture. 9,9 managerial style entails direct confrontation, in which those involved can face up to the conflict, examining and evaluating it under the supervision of the manager. Finally, the effective manager must work through one's own differences with subordinates, recognizing and dealing with their resistances.[18]

One of the most important managerial tasks throughout any endeavor is communication. The manager, at each level, is a key person in the flow of information through the organization. One needs to remain familiar with the major points of progress throughout the performance of a given task. One must present a task or problem, and the information nec-essary to decide a course of action, in language which the subordinate understands. When communication does

87

break down, good management does not view it as the fault of one party or the other, but as a problem of misunderstanding. To increase the degree of openness in communication, the manager must search for and eliminate the problem which causes the lack of openness.[19]

Follow-up

The final stage of any level of development is the follow-up, a mutual evaluation among those who took part in the task. Together they must review and critique each other's past performance, as well as the situation, for the purpose of recognizing both changed and unchanged patterns, discovering new learnings, applying them to future work, and recommending changes. Furthermore, they need to periodically stabilize or support the changes already made by assessing and reinforcing them in order to prevent regression. In fact, from the outset they need to set benchmarks by which to measure progress or slippage.[20]

Adapting The Model

Similarities And Differences

Similarities

At many points the 9,9 business model fits with the Biblical picture of the overseer. Both are advisors, consultants, helpers, and "playing coaches," concerned for the smooth operation of the whole group, the sub-groups, and the supervision of individuals. Both are concerned for order, and take great care to watch for, and respond appropriately to, potential crisis. Both stress the mutual comprehension and acceptance of problems, goals, and means of attaining and evaluating them. In the church, as well as in good business management, each person's unique creativity should find expression, without neglecting shared responsibility and accountability. This demands that church administration provide challenging goals and objectives, opportunity to contribute one's thoughts and energies to an accomplishment, and a sense of recognition and reward.

The church leader's responsibility in this administrative process is not to direct the task, but to work to include others in the process of establishing direction. One needs to coordinate, develop, and supervise others. Furthermore, in the church the same work units and basic strategies exist, though the latter I would call strategies for growth rather than problem-solving strategies. A positive approach seems more appropriate to the church, if not to business as well. Thus the church leader must concern oneself with one's own personal development as an administrator, the supervision of individuals, the development of teams or small groups, and the organizational development of the whole church.

One major advantage to the use of 9,9 business management as a model is the emphasis on people. Yet in the church this emphasis is even greater, since the ultimate aim for production or mission is the growth of persons. Church leadership must discover and utilize individual gifts rather than use persons to fulfill organizational needs. Such substitution of programs for people, of institutional needs for divine purposes, becomes very tempting for the church leader who forgets that the primary calling is that of a servant who is to strengthen and guide, rather than manipulate, the flock.

Differences

Differences do exist between business organizations and the church, making the administrative functions distinct. First, there are differences in the kind of commitment one makes to the church. It is more difficult to gain frequent and steady participation of most people in church programs and activities. The laity are only part-time volunteers, usually serving one year terms of office. This means less stability, less pastoral leverage, and less planning capability, since the pastor does not have any sanction over pay, vacation, or required training. In many churches the leadership has only limited control over promotion within the organization, including the selection of those working closest to them. They do not even have the power to adopt 9,9 managerial style without the consent of the people. In addition, the church's goals are often less definite and frequently perceived as secondary to the job which puts bread on the table. Due to the voluntary nature of lay involvement in the church, it is less likely that all persons will take part in every aspect of decision-making. There is greater resistance to the long process of planning, implementing, and evaluating on the part of people with limited tenure, as well as the freedom to fully decide their degree of involvement.

Ecclesiastical oversight is also unique in that it is not limited in scope to the church organization. We must not neglect the significance of lay ministry through vocational and personal lives. Individuals sent into the secular world can do things that no ecclesiastical institution could accomplish. With more and more women working today, it is imperative that the church leader provide training and oversight to enable all laity to bring the impact of the gospel to the part of the world they touch during their everyday lives. This may call for fewer "church" activities than in the past, or for smaller scale programs. It may mean allowing a lay leader to choose to attend an important meeting of a secular organization even when it conflicts with a church function. Whatever the exact form, it will mean changing the nature of the church and its program from "the gathering point of society" to "the sending point to society," or to adopt an image of the church proposed by Elton Trueblood, from "haven" to "launching pad."[21]

Another unique factor affecting church administration is the comparatively broad nature of the leader's role. Since one is more than just administrator, one can spend only part time doing what the business manager does full time. In addition, the church leader frequently has more people to whom one must relate. The leadership span, the number of people to whom one directly relates, usually exceeds four to eight persons, the number in a typical business firm.[22]

All this implies the need for great care in the selection of the most important supervisory functions. Generally, these functions are the same as for the business manager, planning, work execution, and follow-up. The church leader's unique function is recruiting lay volunteers. Before examining these administrative responsibilities, I will give attention to strategies for growth within each of the work units.

Strategies For Growth In Various Work Units

Personal Development As An Administrator

Since administration plays a part in every task the church leader performs, one's personal development as an administrator is important. Yet, personal development is secondary to team and organizational development because it is the larger group that is ultimately responsible for carrying out the purpose or mission of the church. In fact, personal administrative development may play a diminished role in the low church tradition due to the relatively diminished power or control which the church leader has. One is more of an administrator than a manager. Nevertheless, it is advantageous for the church leader to learn how to function as an individual, as part of a supervisor-subordinate pair, as a team member, and as a member of the whole organization. To do this, one needs to study and understand principles of good administration, factors involved in both intrapersonal and interpersonal dynamics, one's own administrative style, and one's role in relation to the specific congregation one serves.

One of the most essential principles of good administration is time management. In the church administrator's own development, this includes learning to delegate, to budget one's time in a flexible fashion, to use lists which separate the essential from the possible, to organize without being fanatical, to determine one's best work hours, to know when to say "no," to recognize the appropriate form of communication (phone, letter, visit), and to function effectively when one's feelings are caught up in some other concern.

To determine strengths and weaknesses regarding one's own administrative style, one can use various tests available from the business world. Two such instruments, available through Scientific Methods, Inc. of Austin, Texas, are "A Self-examination of Managerial Grid Styles" and "Grid Feedback From A Subordinate to a Boss." In addition, opportunities exist for pastors to assess their administrative styles through dialogue. One such opportunity is the Woodbury Management Workshop, held annually at Andover Newton Theological School in Newton, Massachusetts. Finally, personal feedback from parishioners and/or colleagues can help one see one's own style and growing edges. This evaluation could take place in

91

the context of ongoing church life or in the form of
role play.

Supervision of Individuals

The church leader who wishes to see both personal
and institutional growth within the congregation must
take seriously the task of supervising individuals.
Herein lies a key to the power of the ministry of the
laity, and of the church. One must be willing to
commit oneself to encouraging personal growth, especially regarding a parishioner's ability to perform a
given task. To some extent, the pastor supervises all
persons in the church. However, one cannot possibly do
an adequate job singlehandedly. Consequently, one
must train and supervise certain individuals, leaving
the task of closely supervising others to those with
whom one works. Though it would be most advantageous
to develop such a relationship with the leaders of
existing church groups, in some cases the pastor may
have this kind of relationship with an individual
unaffiliated with any group. These few crucial
leaders in any congregation, whether the designated
officials or others, are the central thrust of ministry, and as such, need the kind of oversight that
Jesus gave to the twelve.

The single most important factor in supervising
these individuals is the relation between supervisor
and supervisee. The supervisor must communicate acceptance, understanding and appreciation, as well as
set high standards for performance. One must also
accept the natural dependence the supervisee is going
to feel, yet without taking away the other's responsibility for learning and growing. Initially, the
supervisor usually needs to be more directive in the
relationship. However, as time goes on, one needs to
involve the supervisee more and more in the task of
self-direction.

The ultimate purpose is to help the supervisee
understand more about self, the ministry situation,
and the future possibilities. To do this, the
supervisor must first help the supervisee to set goals
that are specific, tasks that will lead to fulfillment
of these goals, and criteria for evaluation. The
supervisor must take care to allow the supervisee to
define these from her or his perspective. The supervisor's role is to clarify misconceptions, help set
realistic limits, give recognition for what the
supervisee brings to the situation, and ensure that

the proposed tasks are measurable. Secondly, the supervisor may either work with the supervisee or observe him or her working alone, after which one can help the supervisee to reflect on the experience, especially his or her performance. The supervisor's role is to help the supervisee appropriate potential learning, and handle fears and resistances, both internal and external. Only in rare cases should one remove the person from a task or do it oneself.

This relationship may be very casual, with no regular meetings once the ministry has begun, or it may be very structured. In the first case, the supervisor may well need to take the initiative in checking with the supervisee after two to four weeks, offering one's availability to talk should any problems arise. In the latter case, where growth, rather than crisis intervention, is desired, the supervisor and supervisee need to set definite plans for regular supervision. The frequency will depend on the desires of both persons and the nature of the ministry task. The important thing is that they agree on both the frequency and any tools to be used. Here, it is often beneficial to include written reports as well as a follow-up conference. Yet, when working with certain lay volunteers, it may not be advantageous to suggest that part, or all, of the reporting be written, depending on the degree of motivation and writing skill. One field of ministry which utilizes such a process of regular supervision, focused around written reporting, is the field education of seminary students. This discipline has developed various forms for evaluating skills in observing, leading groups, conversing, etc.[23] Adaptations of these forms may be useful in supervision of lay ministries.

Development of Small Groups

In 9,9 business management, team action is the focal point of concern. So, too, in the church, the small group of six to twelve persons must become the primary place of supervision. Virtually every church has such groups, though they may be informal in nature. These groups not only provide a sense of belonging, but also form the basis for ministry and outreach. Individual gifts are still most effective when expressed through a group of people working together, though one must beware of the danger of cliquishness. Such groups do not include most committees or boards, at least those which deliberate more than act. Instead, they are action groups composed of persons who really want to do something about a given task. These groups need to be given a great deal of freedom of operation, including decisions to form or disband, enter or leave.

The pastor must be concerned with the health of all groups in the church. Yet it is impossible for one person to have a close relationship to each group. To follow Jesus' model, the pastor could band together the lay leaders into a group of their own. This also fits well with 9,9 managerial style, where each person is a member of two teams, one in which he or she leads and one in which he or she is a member. The business model is not completely adequate since the pastor must relate to other groups than this group of leaders, assisting them to understand their function and providing resources and training. However, the more a church can develop a concept of working teams, all under supervision of someone (pastor or lay leader), the healthier is the church. Ideally, the top team should be led by the pastor and be composed of deacons or other lay officials. Yet where these persons lack time or interest, one must search for those persons who have both desire and capability.

The pastor's oversight of the leadership group can serve as a model for these leaders in relation to their own groups. Consequently, the life of this leadership group should include prayer, study, fellowship or support, and evaluation of church, action group, or individual ministries. The role of the pastor is to facilitate the growth of a comfortable atmosphere, where each person is encouraged to draw upon one's own experiences and contribute one's best to the others present. The pastor must help clarify group goals and individual roles, explore resources and opportunities, and evaluate both enabling and blocking forces -- all in a manner that builds team spirit and fosters individual growth. In addition, one may discuss with the group the overall health of the various ministries represented. One may, with permission, bring a particular person's written report to the attention of the whole group for their mutual examination and learning.

Organizational Development

The need still exists for overseeing the ministry of the whole church. There should be a common direction toward which all ministries of a given church are building. The leadership needs to develop an overall

94

plan for congregational life and ministry into which it can place the individuals and groups as they come into existence. At times, the board of elders, deacons or other group responsible for general oversight, may need, for the sake of the health of the congregation, to restrict the areas of concern which the church will address. Yet, at any point, it is vital that the entire church "own" any given action carried on in its name.

In addition to the board which gives general direction, plans and oversees the ministry, many churches, for the sake of distributing responsibility, have a board which is responsible for maintaining the institutional organization and helping implement the established direction for ministry. One way to design this business committee is to include the pastor, all the deacons or elders, leaders of groups or organizations within the church, plus a few representatives at large. This would provide both the spiritual leadership and organizational operation of the church with a variety of perspectives. The pastor would bring his or her own unique view of the whole church life. Each deacon or elder, if given responsibility for overseeing a particular area of church life, such as fellowship, learning, worship, or mission, would bring the concerns of this area to bear on any decisions made. Small group leaders would help focus the business of the church around the church's groups, the heart of its ministry. Representatives at large would contribute their own unique insights and give a sense of representation to those not involved in small groups or organizations. Once formed, this governing board would be wise to delegate, yet supervise, various organizational responsibilities such as finances, property, nominations/personnel, clerical, and publicity. By placing a member of the governing board on any committees responsible for these functions, the church facilitates the process of reporting back and maintaining open communication. By encouraging each person in the congregation to serve in one of these organizational capacities, the necessary maintenance could be done and everyone would still have time for involvement in other functions more central to the purpose of the church. Yet this is only one possible way to provide order, efficiency, and representation to the structure of the church. Each congregation must discover its own best style of organization.

Any design of the church organization involves preparing designs for each group in the church. Representatives of each group need to be present to give input, not only to the design for their own group, but also to the task of spelling out, and working through, the relationship between groups. The final outcome, whatever its form, must, as in business, facilitate open communication, productivity, and the development of ministry capabilities among the membership. The church needs a structure in which various groups can interact naturally and operating tensions can easily come to light.

All this requires pastoral supervision of the governing structures of the entire church. In order to effectively lead the congregation through the process of planning, recruiting, working together, and evaluating, the pastor must accurately perceive the needs of individuals and groups. He or she must also help them to perceive and develop their own ministries. Pastor and lay leadership need to creatively involve as many people as possible in the administrative process in order to best facilitate the unity and mission of the church. Like the 9,9 business manager, church administrators must foster a team spirit in which no one loses and everyone wins, that the church might grow into the true community it was meant to be.

Responsibilities of the Church Administrator

Most of these responsibilities (planning, recruiting, work execution, and follow-up) are applicable to the church administrator's relationships within each of the work units.

Planning

Each work unit must plan in order to organize the work execution and any necessary recruitment, and to design the follow-up. However, the plans of the larger work unit will always influence those beneath it. All levels must tailor their planning to fit the needs of individuals, providing a unique, challenging, and fruitful role for each person. Sometimes, for the sake of decisiveness, this planning needs to be done by one or a few persons in leadership. However, even in these cases, there should be some provision for input from persons with relevant facts or a stake in the outcome. When planning for the whole institution, the deacons or elders seem to be the most logical group to provide this function, given their responsibility of oversight for the whole church's ministry. Yet a planning committee could serve this function, perhaps in conjunction with the church leadership. However it is structured, the group primarily responsible for the process should usually seek to include the whole congregation in some aspect of the planning through surveys, open discussion, or informal listening.

The role of the church leader in this endeavor is to help people see the need for planning, and then consult with the persons leading the process in order to ensure that appropriate persons are included and good plans are made. To enable people to recognize the need for planning, the pastor or lay leader can provide experiences which assist them to perceive problems and dream dreams. Furthermore, one can carefully study and present the benefits to the appropriate person or body, and discuss the matter during pastoral visits or at meetings of small groups. One thing one should not do is prepare ahead a specific plan.

To develop good plans, those involved need to identify the purposes (not just the problems as in 9,9 management), analyze the situation, devise alternative solutions, decide the best course of action, set out the steps to be taken and assign responsibilities for implementation. To identify good purposes, one may take problems and convert them into possibilities. To effectively analyze the situation entails careful examination of the needs and resources inherent within individuals, church groups, and the surrounding neighborhood. To devise alternative solutions, any involved in the planning may share all conceivable possibilities, and then analyze each proposal, noting advantages and disadvantages. To arrive at the best course of action, it is helpful to arrange the alternatives in order of desirability, and recognize that more than one of them may be useful. To determine the specific steps, one should place priorities upon the various events which need to happen and decide which events can take place independently and which must happen concurrently. To make appropriate assignments, each person, to the extent possible, should be asked to take a unique and challenging part. It must stimulate their interest and comprise a complete step in the process, so one can see results from one's labor.

Recruitment

Despite the fact that recruitment is not included in 9,9 management, it is always a very important administrative task for any volunteer organization. Only the higher-level work units, small groups and the whole organization, need to do recruitment. The process is usually an informal one in the former, but somewhat more complicated in the latter. In either case, all the leadership in the group or congregation should take an active part. In the small group this usually means the group leader, if there is one, and perhaps other members or the pastor. In the whole congregation, this should involve the pastor and lay leadership as well as members of the nominating and/or personnel committee(s). All these persons must participate in selecting and inviting people to perform certain specific tasks.

It is important to be selective in choosing persons for any task, for God does not distribute gifts equally to all persons, or all gifts to any one person. Those responsible must evaluate each person and his or her gifts. However, they should be able to include everyone at some point. In fact, it may be important to make sure that the various segments of the church have representation on certain committees or groups. They should take into account age, sex, race, class, and natural social groupings. Given this attention to the needs for diversity, one should then look for persons with a sense of enthusiasm for, purpose in, and calling to, the particular task. This does not imply that only those with great leadership qualities can serve. Estimation of a person's potential must also be a factor.

One task of the church leadership is to regularly review the list of church members and friends to discover people who would do well in a variety of responsibilities. Many of these may be approached directly by an individual leader. A more formal approach is to have the nominating committee distribute to the whole congregation a survey to obtain information concerning a person's past and present services as well as interests. In this way, people gain input into the process which will determine their areas of service. Such a form might include church offices, other elected positions, and existing, or proposed, committees, action groups, church programs, or mission projects. Finally, the committee can evaluate persons themselves, either by interviewing or watching their performance on certain tasks. In fact, it may be wise to involve new persons in special, temporary projects in order to see how well they function. Furthermore, one should not forget to look at someone's vocation or membership in secular organizations for clues to potential leadership abilities. It is not always wise, though, to have a person do exactly the same function within the church that one does in the secular world. The purposes of the church are different.

Once they have all this input, the committee members can then make their individual suggestions. They may list both those who they feel are ready to actively serve in a certain capacity and those who have potential to serve effectively. When they have gathered these suggestions, they must then ask which persons have the needed qualities or experience, the ability to work together, or too many other commitments. Finally, they need to make specific nominations for elected positions and pass on information or recommendations to the leadership regarding non-elective responsibilities.

The persons selected must then be invited to accept the responsibility. This function may fall to any number of people, depending on the nature of the responsibility. The pastor or an elder/deacon should approach any person regarding small group leadership or the initiation of a new ministry. A member of the nominating committee should approach potential committee members. Small group leaders may approach members of their group for special tasks or contact potential members regarding joining. Usually it is better to visit rather than phone, and to use the occasion to explore the other's sense of calling. Whoever extends the invitation should clearly spell out the responsibilities involved, availability of special training, any time framework, and the nature of any accountability.

Work Execution

Once people have accepted assignments to particular tasks, the pastor and lay leadership are responsible to see that the person or group executes the task well. They must take the lead in directing, coordinating and communicating. In addition, they must, at times, re-enlist or re-energize persons due to the voluntary nature of lay involvement in the church.

The responsibility of providing direction involves helping the appropriate people understand who needs to participate in performing the task, see the implications of the proposal, and gain the confidence and ability to perform adequately. To do this, one must encourage experimentation, do on-the-job supervision, and take measures to prevent or remove obstacles.

The task of coordinating and communicating is an essential part of the administrative task in any of the work units. In this capacity the pastor and lay leaders are the key to the flow of information. As such it is up to them to foster team spirit, where each person feels at home and contributes one's best. They must show concern and understanding by informing the people of their availability to consult with all concerned. They must communicate with language and manner which all comprehend. They are often responsible for presenting proposed changes to the appropriate individual or group, and seeing that they understand the proposed objective and strategy. They must always be familiar with the points of progress, the interpersonal dynamics, and the available resources. Finally, they must be willing and able to moderate conflict, including differences among themselves and between themselves and others. They must be good listeners, yet know when a person needs, and can face, direct confrontation. They need to avoid laying blame on any one party for the breakdown of communication, viewing it, instead, as a problem of misunderstanding. They must help people search for, and eliminate, the problems which cause the conflict. At last, after conflict occurs, it is important for the pastor to re-enlist and re-energize the person(s), persuading and motivating them to continue in service.

Follow-up

Follow-up can take place within any of the work units. Its purpose is to determine the degree of actualization of goals, recognizing both changed and unchanged patterns of behavior, discovering new learnings, applying them to future work, and recommending changes.

Some degree of evaluation is an ongoing procedure within each step of the administrative process. Follow-up, however, is intentional evaluation at a specific point in time. It can be either a short process at a group's conclusion of a specific task, or a longer one when a congregation is re-examining its entire program. If possible, all who take part in the task should be part of this process. However, when the work unit is the whole congregation and the task is not a major one, the group responsible for planning may perform the better portion of this function.

Whether long-term or short-term, those involved must critique the performance of each person and review the situation. To critique personal performance, there must be clear criteria set out at the beginning of the task. Even then, this is difficult. There is often a discrepancy between espoused and actual changes in behavior. The espoused change may reflect a change in awareness and aspiration, but not in behavior itself. This consciousness-raising is important, but must be recognized for what it is. Over a short time period this may be all that is possible. Yet one must keep in mind that the ultimate purpose is to affect performance, not just awareness.

To review the whole situation and make necessary changes in goals, strategies, or tactics, each person must present one's perception of any problems or successes, and recommend improvements of the goals, strategies or tactics. To do this in a large group it may be necessary to visually record each person's input. Finally, they must ask what they can do to make necessary improvements and reinforce those actions and activities which proved fruitful.

Throughout this process of critiquing performance, reviewing the situation, and adjusting goals, strategy, and tactics, all parties must take care to emphasize the positive. This process should provide everyone with a sense of gratification, even if it is only that of learning how to avoid a mistake.

Summary

The church administrator concerns oneself with planning, recruitment, work execution, and follow-up within all the work units of the church. He or she utilizes each of the strategies for growth in one's own development as an administrator, the supervision of individuals, the development of small groups, and the development of the whole organization.

To develop one's own administrative abilities, the effective administrator studies the principles

behind good administration (especially time management), the dynamics of relationships, one's own
administrative style, and one's role in the specific
congregation. To effectively supervise individuals
the pastor needs to meet casually with many persons
and regularly with a handful of persons, preferably
those who are leaders of groups within the church and
can, in turn, supervise the rest of the laity. One
must help the individual to set goals, tasks and
criteria for evaluation, as well as reflect on his or
her performance. Yet one's relationship with the
individual is the most important factor. To develop
small groups, the primary work unit in the church, the
pastor can utilize the same team concept as in 9,9
management. One can lead a team of action group
leaders, assisting them and their groups to grow and
to minister effectively. To effectively organize the
whole church, all segments of the church must be
appropriately involved in organizational redesign and
examination of any tensions. The resulting organization should be one that facilitates open communication, productivity, and development of parishioners'
ministry capabilities.

Finally, the church leader must see that each of
the administrative tasks are performed well. To lead
in the planning, one must assist people to recognize
the need for it and make sure that appropriate persons
are included at least indirectly. Then one needs to
help identify purposes, analyze the situation, devise
alternative solutions, decide on the best one, set out
the steps in the process, and make appropriate assignments. In all this, one must see to it that each
individual receives a unique and fitting task. To
facilitate recruitment, the church leader needs to
continually help people discover their gifts. He or
she may approach individuals directly or work with a
nominating committee to discern potential or actual
callings and invite persons to commitment. To supervise the work execution, the church administrator
needs to lead in directing the task by helping the
people understand who needs to participate in performing the activity, the implications of the proposal for
each individual, and how to gain confidence and
ability. One has to take the lead in coordinating the
activities and maintaining open communication between
individuals and groups. At times, one must re-enlist
and re-motivate persons who have become disillusioned.
To follow-up the endeavor, the church leader has to
assist the laity to evaluate intentionally their
goals, behavior, and learnings as well as recommend

changes.   When possible, all those involved in the task should critique the performance of each person, review the situation, and adjust their goals, strategies, and tactics.   This involves much more than simply noting an increased awareness of the problem. In this entire process, one must continually stress the positive, as commendation goes much further than judgment.

NOTES

1. Robert R. Blake and Jane Srygley Mouton, *The Managerial Grid: Key Orientations For Achieving Productivity Through People* (Houston, Texas: Gulf Publishing Co., 1964), p. 223.

2. *Ibid.*, pp. 143 and 296.

3. *Ibid.*, p. 146.

4. Robert R. Blake and Jane Srygley Mouton, *Building A Dynamic Corporation Through Grid Organization Development*, Addison-Wesley Series on Organization Development (Reading, Massachusetts: Addison-Wesley Publishing Company, 1969), pp. 68 and 114.

5. Blake and Mouton, *The Managerial Grid*, pp. 147, 166 and 173.

6. *Ibid.*, pp. 148, 153, 170, 270 and 304.

7. *Ibid.*, pp. 154-156.

8. Robert R. Blake, Jane S. Mouton, Louis B. Barnes, and Larry E. Greiner, "Breakthrough In Organizational Development," *Harvard Business Review* (November-December, 1964), p. 137.

9. Robert R. Blake and Jane Srygley Mouton, *The Grid For Supervisory Effectiveness* (Austin, Texas: Scientific Methods, Inc., 1975), pp. 102 and 106.

10. Blake and Mouton, *Building A Dynamic Corporation*, pp. 84-85.

11. Robert Blake and Jane Srygley Mouton, *Corporate Excellence Through Grid Organizational Development* (Houston, Texas: Gulf Publishing Co., 1968), pp. 239 and 242.

12. Blake, Mouton, Barnes, and Greiner, "Breakthrough In Organizational Development," p. 138.

13. Peter F. Drucker, *Management: Tasks, Responsibilities, Practices* (New York: Harper and Row, Publishers, 1973), pp. 121-125.

14. Blake and Mouton, The Managerial Grid, pp. 143, 151, 274, and 308.

15. Blake, Mouton, Barnes, and Greiner, "Breakthrough In Organizational Development," p. 138.

16. Peter Drucker, The Practice of Management (New York: Harper, 1954), pp. 295-298.

17. Blake, Mouton, Barnes, and Greiner, "Breakthrough In Organizational Development," p. 138.

18. Blake and Mouton, The Managerial Grid, pp. 143, 152, and 163-165.

19. Ibid., pp. 143 and 157-161.

20. Blake and Mouton, Building A Dynamic Corporation, pp. 73-74, 87, and 108-109.

21. D. Elton Trueblood, The Company of the Committed (New York: Harper and Row, 1961), pp. 72-73.

22. Arthur Adams, Pastoral Administration (Philadelphia: Westminster Press, 1964), pp. 46-47.

23. George Hunter, Theological Field Education (Newton Centre, Massachusetts: The Boston Theological Institute, 1977), pp. 168-174; and

Thomas W. Klink, "Supervision As A Routine Process In Professional Education for Ministry," (Typewritten paper reprinted in the Duke Divinity School Review, 1968), pp. 5-13.

CHAPTER VI

TEACHING

The best secular parallel for the function of teaching comes from the field of education. One cannot apply all trends in the modern teaching profession to the church. Yet the basic heuristic approach of today's secular education does have much to offer.

The Heuristic Approach To Education

Experience and Discovery

The heuristic approach emphasizes the personal discovery and experience of the student as the central focus of teaching, yet without neglecting the significance of content.[1]

The Place of Experience And Content

According to heuristic theory, one learns best when one experiences something. This includes utilizing both past and present experiences, or structuring the educational context so it provides new ones. The learner needs someone or something to stir one to search for new insights and fit them together into a coherent body of thought.[2] This kind of discovery process enables the student to choose for oneself and, thus, truly "own" the learning.

The emphasis on experience arose in recent times due to a sense that education no longer related to life. Students seemed unable to apply, or even remember, content presented to them. Yet in the early stages, this new approach went to the opposite extreme. It ignored academic content under the guise of relevance to life. More recently the emphasis has shifted back toward content, yet with concern for its relationship to experience.[3]

Today, heuristic education begins with experience, moves toward abstraction, then returns to experience. One must introduce new material through a person's own discovery process. However one must then move the student away from obviousness and superficial experience by presenting content. Content provides a set of principles and concepts which form a structure within which we can better integrate and understand experience. It also provides alternative views and has the potential for creating new interests. Finally, after formulating these principles, concepts, and viewpoints, it is of paramount importance to apply this content back to life experiences.[4]

The Role Of The Teacher

The heuristic teacher must anticipate, but not prejudice, the learning process. The primary concern should be the development of self-direction on the part of the student. Consequently, one should place most questions and initiatives back in the student's lap. Yet, one must still be somewhat directive, for people need to be led through this learning process. The teacher's task is to provide the learner with materials and tools, necessary for the discovery and integration of experience.[5] This, one does in the context of the school, that special community whose very purpose is to help one experience discovery.

As a leader in the learning process, the teacher must proceed with gradual steps, since behavior changes slowly. Students need time to restate and practice, in order for permanent change to take place. The teacher must also provide input at a time when the student is most ready. The teacher must solicit, and listen to, both verbal and non-verbal feedback, that he or she might respond appropriately. One must learn from students, accept any resistances to change, help students learn from failure, utilize outside resource people, and provide adequate emotional support. In all this, one needs to be secure in one's own person and subject matter, and model for the student the pursuit of excellence.[6]

Methods of Instruction

To achieve this type of instruction many strategies for presenting material are appropriate. Some students will respond better to an inductive approach, others to a deductive one. Consequently, varying formats, such as lecture, explanation followed by practice, small seminar, reading, and private study are all equally valid. The teacher must determine which method to use on the basis of the student's capacity to utilize the learning opportunity.

Adaptive Education

One common method for achieving the goals of heuristic education is the individualization of instruction. Here the principal concern is not the discipline, but the student and his or her acquisition of a small number of easily identifiable skills or facts. The student determines for oneself what, when, and how quickly, he or she studies. The teacher merely removes obstacles and provides a conducive environment.[7] Recently, however, many are questioning this method due to insufficient student motivation, inability of the student to discern the best approach, and added teacher workload.

Adaptive education is a modification of individualized instruction. It differs in that the teacher must tailor subject matter presentations to fit the special requirements and capabilities of each learner. Consequently, it still involves a large investment of time, limiting the number of people one can teach through this method. The most significant factor in determining an adaptive program of education is one's past history of responses within educational settings. The adaptive approach assumes that everyone learns best if the teacher provides rewards, giving each his or her most preferred type of reinforcement. For some this means encouragement in the form of approval, for others the receiving of tokens, for others a high rating in competition.[8]

Group Work

Another method of instruction common today is group work, which involves a large number of persons whom the instructor divides into subgroups for the sake of better dialogue. It is wise for the teacher to use indigenous leadership in these groups, giving them jurisdiction to handle all but the most difficult problems. Subgrouping is an excellent way to start discussion that enhances the learning of the whole group. It gives a person the chance to rehearse something and gain support for one's ideas. In addition, subgroups provide opportunity for clarification of issues, working through unhelpful attitudes, consultation and decision-making, feedback and evaluation. The teacher's role is to keep one's finger on all that transpires. By moving around to the various

109

groups, one can get a feel for what is happening, ask a question or challenge something, get to know individuals, and call time more sensitively. In no case should one do the work for the group.[9]

A variation of this approach is the small group seminar. It differs from the subgroup in that it is not part of a larger unit to which it must immediately report. It also has more organization and larger numbers. If an educational institution decides to use a seminar structure, then it needs small group leaders in addition to the primary teacher. The small group leaders, then, may comprise a group of their own, led by the head teacher, for the purpose of enabling them to better lead their groups.[10]

Adapting The Model

Similarities And Differences

Similarities

Revelation, by definition, is the experience of being encountered by God's Spirit, discovering the greatest of all truths. It involves the recognition of God as part of, indeed creator and Lord of, the environment with which one interacts. It is much more than head knowledge. It is experience-based understanding. Furthermore, it is not a one time event, but a lifelong process, encompassing each moment, each thought, each activity. The heart of the gospel has to do with life and experience, decision and response. The aim of Christian education, then, becomes the assimilation and integration of all the experiences God offers, incorporating them in such a way that they affect all of one's actions. The early church demonstrated such an understanding of its educational purpose by its ritualistic recounting of past experiences, its continually expectant posture, and its eagerness to share with others each new discovery. Therefore we may conclude that the heuristic approach of discovery and experience, both past and present, may suit Christian education even better than its secular counterpart.

Another emphasis the church shares with secular heuristic education is the building of community. Heuristic education encourages a dialogue approach to teaching in order to establish bonds between people. One can also use this approach in a variety of settings with diverse kinds of people, for example, those preferring a deductive, or an inductive, approach.

In light of these similarities it makes sense to examine the place of experience, the place of content, and the place of adaption to the individual, with regard to both teaching and preaching in the church. However, before going on, it is important to clarify some differences between church and secular contexts in order to adapt the model most appropriately.

Differences

The task of motivation, a key to the effectiveness of the heuristic approach, is more difficult in the church than in secular education. Even the most open of secular classrooms has a greater degree of built-in pressure to accomplish certain educational goals and finish the educational process. Despite the low key approach, society still automatically rewards, and in some cases requires, this education. The existence of the school, as a special place of instruction with specific time commitments, helps to create this higher motivation. The church might well take seriously the advantages of creating more specificity over place and time of instruction, whether it be the church school or the home Bible study. The issue is not which time block or place becomes special, but that one becomes special. Furthermore, Christian education improves if one designates a terminal point for each educational unit. When one fails to do this, it thwarts the opportunity to conclude one stage of instruction and move on to another. This calls, then, for specific covenants of learning between teacher and student.

A second major difference between church and secular contexts is that older persons are usually present in the church. This heterogeneity requires greater attention to the kinds of stimulation necessary to motivate adults. The church makes a grave mistake when it patterns itself too much after secular methods of motivation designed primarily for children. An important question facing the church teacher is how to stir people when the explosive, inquisitive years of childhood and youth are over.

The Place of Experience

Until recently, teachers of the faith have stressed correct verbalization of truth rather than the living of it. The church utilized a very directive approach to teaching and preaching that carried over into the entirety of ministry as seen in the Reformation period. More recently the church has begun to see the task of Christian education as the provision of experiences which will produce character and attitudinal change, as well as develop understanding and skills in ministry.

The heuristically oriented church leader needs to ensure that one's parishioners gain the opportunity to have experiences that enhance growth. This means one must have a good grasp of the particular learner's stage of development and be able to guide the person through the learning process. Yet one must not attempt to control all the circumstances, for personal responsibility for learning should always rest on the learner.

To effectively guide a person's learning, the teacher/preacher has to order the steps in the educational process, spacing the material so that the parishioner may gain maximum benefit. One has to search for the right materials to provide certain needed experiences, the right format to achieve a desired effect, or the right opportunity for the parishioner to restate and practice new learnings. One must seek out, and heed, both verbal and non-verbal feedback, accepting any criticism or resistance, and providing needed emotional support. In order to produce this kind of teaching environment, the pastor or lay leader needs to model for the parishioners the posture of a learner and embody the message one wishes to communicate. When a person can speak of what one has seen and heard and learned, when he/she can speak from the heart as well as from the mind, then the preaching or teaching is fresh, exciting and authentic. This requires a good sense of personal and professional security and self-confidence, for it involves revealing oneself. Consequently, the preacher/teacher has to prepare oneself personally even more than one prepares the sermon or class. Finally, the pastor or lay leader who is secure and confident is free to utilize outside persons as resources in both the preparation of instructional material and the teaching/preaching itself. We need to make better use of persons on the frontiers of discovery, in both articulation and application of Christian faith, especially in secular settings.

Teaching

Discovery ought to be the focus of any Christian teaching. Occasionally, the primary subject matter can be experience, as in encounter groups. Or one can study the life of another person, such as a Biblical character, with which the parishioner can identify. Still another alternative is to tie in with the parishioner's own prior or ongoing, experiences. Finally, like Jesus, one can even use demonstration or proclamation in such a way as to create, or tie in with, a parishioner's experience.

The focus on experience affects the approach to all forms of Christian teaching. The teacher needs to start with a format familiar to parishioners and adopt new methods only when enough people are ready for them. Second, one must give parishioners responsibility for their own learning by placing most questions back in the lap of the seeker. Third, she/he needs to demonstrate a teachableness in one's own life, especially in settings with which other people are far more familiar. Fourth, one must structure in the feedback, whether informally at the end of a small discussion group, or by use of evaluation forms and sessions after a large group has just completed an involved learning process. Finally, one must keep in mind the need for practice. For example, in teaching on prayer it is not enough to read or expound a passage from the Bible. The learner needs to observe others, write out prayers, and take part in both private and corporate prayer, again and again.

Preaching

Preaching should provide an experience of the presence and power of God. Consequently, it needs to be vivid, moving, and dramatic, without becoming a performance. It is an oral event or experience among preacher, parishioner, and God.

The sermon is primarily a proclamation from God to the parishioner, an announcement of what God has done and is doing. It is to be a message of "experienceable" good news. In this light, the preacher should not simply tell people to live better, for this only builds a sense of recurrent failure and hopelessness.

113

The preacher must also experience the activity of God in order to provide such an encounter for the parishioner. To be convincing, everything a preacher says must be demonstrated in one's life. Good preaching, then, involves revealing one's own struggle to live with God.

Preaching entails dialogue between preacher and parishioner as well as divine-human encounter. The preacher must demonstrate a willingness to learn. He/she needs to accept the responses of the listeners, regardless of what they may be. What is clear to the preacher may not always be so obvious to the person in the pew. This listening can enhance relationships and deepen a person's response to the gospel.

To create an oral event, preaching must touch base with the life experiences of the parishioners. The preacher must sensitively ascertain the needs in the congregation, choose topics accordingly, speak in a language and style which will communicate effectively, and include specific, concrete application of one's points. To facilitate appropriation of this preaching, one can provide opportunities to respond to the Word -- symbolically within the worship service, or actively in one's daily life. The preacher may provide the stimulus to restate and practice the good news through such means as: formal or informal sharing following the sermon, suggested activities or assignments within the bulletin, and sensitive interaction during visits.

The Place of Content

Despite the emphasis on experience, church teaching, like secular education, cannot neglect content. One needs the integrating framework of doctrinal understanding to give meaning to the network of raw experience. The gaining of a new perspective can give needed structure to the discovery process of Christian growth. Consequently, the preacher/teacher must think through what experiences one is trying to fit together and what doctrinal or theological structure is needed to give meaning and integration. Secondly, this content provides alternative views which come from outside one's own experience. The Scriptures, for example, present such an objective perspective in both preaching and teaching. As in both secular heuristic education and the Biblical pattern, the task involves a constant interplay between two types of instruction, the cognitive teaching of faith or doctrine and the more experiential instruction of conduct. The teacher or preacher is responsible to stir the body of learners, the church, to willingly investigate new areas of discovery and thereby grow toward a mature understanding and living of the great Christian truths.

Teaching

Certainly, today's church leadership must present the content of contemporary Christian education in a much different manner than the mechanical approach of the old catechisms. Most important is the need to tie in the content with experience. Asking parishioners to help select a topic for study is one way to achieve this. In addition, sensitivity to needs and points of application in individual lives is crucial. One method which can help facilitate this identification with experience is the inductive approach to study of the Bible or other literature. Rather than lecture on a particular passage or theme, the teacher, here, leads a discussion by asking questions: "What does it say?", "What does it mean?", and "How can I apply it to my life?". The first two of these questions introduce the content, which hopefully can provide new perspectives, viewpoints, information and understanding, as well as stimulate new interests. Finally, the last question returns to the level of application. Whatever the method, it is important to summarize the issues at hand or the new learnings just realized.

Preaching

The experience-to-abstraction-to-experience pattern should apply to preaching as well as other areas of Christian education. Though preaching involves discovery, it is also one of the best forms for providing the faith framework for one's life. In preaching, one has the advantage of being able to pull together and integrate experiences more directly and to introduce alternative perspectives. One has, beforehand, the chance to think out how a particular doctrinal or Biblical understanding can shed light on certain issues. Preaching affords the best opportunity to carefully work out one's content, whereas informal, discussion-oriented teaching provides the best opportunity to identify with experience. Consequently, when preaching loses a sense of its place in the development of doctrinal understanding, and becomes merely inspirational, its primary value is undercut and it deteriorates. We can conclude that, due to the sermon's monological format, one can best use it to provide faith integration which can give new insight into previous experiences.

In this light, the preacher should not frequently use the sermon as a primary tool for raising controversial issues. Such an approach works counter to the unique thrust of integration. Instead, one can best use preaching to reinforce and restructure already existing attitudes, make explicit those which are held tacitly, and help people to see implications of positions they already accept. Perhaps one can influence the parishioner on issues where she/he has not yet formulated fixed positions by outlining a vision or introducing new information.[11]

The Place Of Adaptation To the Individual

In light of the fact that the heuristic approach emphasizes the need for individual ownership, Christian education must help the parishioner to own his/her decisions regarding Christian discipleship. The preacher/teacher needs to help the parishioner to investigate for oneself the Lordship of Christ and incorporate the call to discipleship into one's own life. To accomplish this, Christian education must adapt to the individual's needs, capabilities, prior achievements, and responses within educational settings. This involves a degree of self-direction on the part of the parishioner. However, the preacher/teacher must do more than merely remove obstacles to learning. One must tailor the educational program to fit each person. To do this one must determine the starting point and the amount, and method, of presenting new input or experience. Like the secular heuristic educator, one may need to proceed faster or slower, with shorter or longer steps, with more practical or more theological material, or by limiting, or directing attention toward, the addition of new material.

In order to tailor the education, the preacher/teacher must use, as the primary guideline, the parishioner's capacity to utilize any given experience. One needs to be very selective in choice of materials, not bringing every related fact into a sermon or discussion. Such compulsion only serves to distract from learning. In addition, good Christian education requires individually tailored reinforcement. Since different things motivate different people, gifts and certificates may be a perfectly valid reward system for some, while others need other kinds of approval and personal encouragement.

Teaching

Individualized adaptation obviously works best when teaching only one person. At times, this one-to-one approach may be important to achieve the degree of adaptation necessary for a particular individual. For example, the teacher can help someone to choose appropriate devotional material by presenting an assortment of possibilities, all selected with the individual's own needs and experiences in mind. Usually, though, a teacher can adequately individualize the learning by spending some time with individuals alone in the context of a group educational experience. Such a group setting provides experiences any parishioner needs for personal growth. Thus one can achieve an optimum balance of interpersonal experience and individual adaptability through the use of small groups.

The small group context provides participants a good opportunity to identify problems or issues, to question one another, to brainstorm together, to give mutual feedback and support, and to practice their learnings. All these interactions become means by which the parishioners can help to individually tailor the learning experience for one another. Yet, in addition, the teacher must attempt to adapt the learning to individuals. One way to do this is to select the right opportunity to provide certain teaching. For example, the experience of new birth becomes the occasion for instruction about baptism. The experience of becoming a church school teacher or Bible study leader is a good opportunity for specialized training. Countless other experiences provide the chance for the church leader to offer various special workshops or growth groups. The alert leader attempts to assess the points of need most apparent among the people and formulate a teaching program around these needs.

Even in large group teaching situations some church school programs have demonstrated how to individualize instruction through subgrouping.[12] One could use a similar format for adults. In this context, the teacher has the chance to move among the groups, to get the feel of what is happening, to

117

question and challenge. This provides one with further advantage in the task of individually tailoring the instruction, while providing the opportunity to foster a sense of community at the same time.

Preaching

Of the various tasks related to teaching, preaching is probably the least suited to individual adaptation. Yet it is important for the preacher, prophet, or evangelist to individually tailor one's message as much as possible. The preacher needs to remember that each listener hears the sermon as an individual, not as a whole congregation. Moreover, one has to recognize that preaching should take place not only because the preacher has something to say, but primarily because the parishioner is ready to hear. The preacher's task is not only to give the message, but to make it possible for the parishioner to wrestle with the message. One must be willing, at points, to even sacrifice one's own preconceived notions of "correct understandings" or "good preaching" in order to address the parishioners at a point where they can hear.

To do this, the preacher has to enter into the parishioner's frame of reference during both the preparation and the preaching itself. During the sermon, one must attempt to pick up, and assimilate quickly, the parishioner's non-verbal responses -- facial expressions, posture, bodily movements, etc. Prior to the actual preaching, one needs to judge the capacity of individuals within the congregation to utilize the encounter with the particular Word. Furthermore, one must take care to draw out applications which bring things to bear on individual lives. Too often, prophetic preaching has become a denunciation of personal or social evils, for which the only application becomes a vague implication of individual responsibility. Only when the preacher addresses the question of what the parishioner can do, or how God has provided us with grace and strength to face the problem, can the parishioner appropriate the Word.

To adapt one's preaching to a majority of the individuals in one's congregation, the preacher must gain an understanding of the general class of people in the congregation -- their ways of looking at and coping with life, the social pressures which influence them, and the self-identification they possess as a people. To assist in the process of individually

118

tailoring a specific part of a sermon to a particular set of people, the preacher may wish to keep in mind certain individuals while preparing and delivering the message.

Summary

Any Christian teaching or preaching must be an experience which stirs the parishioner to search for new insights and fit them together into a coherent structure. Whether given to groups or individuals, it must begin at the level of present experience, then provide the content necessary to integrate and inform experience, and finally return to a point of application for life. The teacher/preacher's principal task in this educational process is to see that learning takes place, yet without removing the parishioner's responsibility for one's own learning. To accomplish this, one must be somewhat directive, yet primarily a cultivator of self-direction. One must help the parishioner to own the learning by adapting it to individual needs. The teacher/preacher's function is to provide emotional support, to demonstrate an attitude of teachableness, and embody the learning. The primary focus in preparation needs to be oneself, not the material.

When applied to teaching, this focus requires a great deal of parishioner participation in the learning process. However, demonstration and proclamation also are useful for creating new experiences, identifying with the experiences of others, or tying in with a parishioner's prior, or on-going, experience. Despite this emphasis, content is still necessary to provide integration and new information or perspectives. To identify content with experience an inductive approach is helpful when studying literature. Yet, whatever the method, the teacher needs to summarize and apply any new learnings. Finally, this teaching requires individual adaptation or tailoring, either one-to-one or within small groups. The latter, though, provides the best balance between adaptability to the individual and provision for interpersonal dialogue.

Preaching can also be experience-based, despite its usual monological format. It should be dramatic, without becoming a performance; it is an oral event, between preacher, parishioner, and God. To create such an oral event, the sermon should begin and end at the level of experience. Yet preaching is also the most appropriate forum of consciously structuring or integrating parishioners' understanding of faith. Thus the kind of oral event it can best produce is one of reinforcing, restructuring, making explicit, or applying existing attitudes, rather than raising controversial issues. Finally, the preacher must attempt to adapt the message to individuals. To do this, one must enter into the frame of reference of the parishioner during both preparation and delivery. One may wish to keep in mind certain individuals while preaching, in addition to gaining an understanding of the general class of people in the congregation.

1.   Leslie Button, <u>Discovery And Experience</u> (London: Oxford University Press, 1971), p. 3.

2.   <u>Ibid.</u>, pp. 19 and 112.

3.   Mauritz Johnson, "The Rise and Fall of 'Life Adjustment,'" in <u>American Education Today</u>, ed. by Paul Woodring and John Scanlon (4th ed.; New York: McGraw-Hill Book Company, Inc., 1963), pp. 52-56.

4.   Jerome Bruner, "After John Dewey, What?," in <u>American Education Today</u>, ed. by Paul Woodring and John Scanlon (4th ed.; New York: McGraw-Hill Book Company, Inc., 1963), pp. 46-48.

5.   Button, pp. 112-113, 124 and 129.

6.   <u>Ibid.</u>, pp. 16-17, 49, 59-60, 124, 137, and 178.

7.   Harold Mitzel, "The Impending Instruction Revolution," in <u>Individualized Instruction And Learning</u>, compiled and edited by Madan Mohan and Ronald Hull (Chicago: Nelson Hall Co., 1974), pp. 70-71.

8.   <u>Ibid.</u>, pp. 71-75.

9.   Button, pp. 96 and 123-125.

10.   <u>Ibid.</u>, pp. 132 and 156.

11.   David E. Babin, <u>Week In - Week Out: A New Look At Liturgical Preaching</u> (New York: The Seabury Press, 1976), p. 43.

12.   Francis Eastman, "The Open Church School," in <u>A Colloquy On Christian Education</u>, ed. by John Westerhoff III (Philadelphia: United Church Press, 1972), pp. 106-111.

CHAPTER VII

CARE

Throughout church history, as noted in chapter 3, the physician was an important model for the shepherd's care of the flock. In addition, Jesus, the Great Shepherd, was a healer. Therefore, it makes sense to look to a contemporary medical model to find some direction for church leaders in this area.

The best contemporary medical model is that of the family physician. Family practice is a specialty in breadth instead of depth. It focuses on the family unit as well as the sick individual, and concentrates on health rather than disease.[1]

The Family Physician

The uniqueness of family practice lies in the physician's familiarity with, and acceptance of, the patient's environment and the family's strengths and limitations. One must be sensitive to expectations and emotions, on the part of oneself, the patient, the family, and the entire community. Empathy, compassion, and flexibility should distinguish one's practice.[2]

Two identifying characteristics of family practice are comprehensiveness and continuity of care. "Comprehensive medical care implies direct service over broad areas of medicine and the availability of this to all patients. Continuity of care implies that the doctor will accept overall responsibility for the patient's care over extended periods of time."[3] Most patients of family physicians have common diseases. Yet one must still have a knowledge of the more chronic illnesses and various methods of treating them, especially in the absence of specialists. When a specialist does see a patient, the family physician can facilitate access to the whole health care system, while never abandoning the person. In addition to patient care functions, comprehensive and continuous care necessitates coordination of health care and concern for its quality in the community.[4]

Patient Care Functions

The patient care functions of the family physician include diagnosis, preventive medicine, therapy, rehabilitation, and referral.[5]

Diagnosis

The family physician must sort out patients by administering a process of data collection. Primarily this involves interviewing persons to discover their medical history. It is important to obtain this data as soon as possible, and to periodically update the record.[6]

As the family physician enters the interview, one must begin with the patient's "presenting problem" and discover the predominant feeling the patient has in relation to this symptom. The physician should then seek to understand the situation which evoked this feeling and clarify one's understanding of the patient's present and past behavior. To do all this, it is very important to put primary value on the input of the patient. Yet one must also establish a contract with the patient, an agreement to relate to each other, exchange information, and give and receive treatment. To gain the most information, the physician needs to ask questions which help patients tell their stories, and make every effort to understand accurately the patient's use of certain words. At times, one needs to focus on items of importance to get more information or to clarify. Finally, one should summarize and/or prescribe some action.[7]

Preventive Medicine

The aim of preventive medicine is to avert the occurrence, or delay the progression, of disease at any stage.[8] This requires the family physician to be a health teacher. One must help persons recognize danger signals and assist parents in the healthy development of children by providing useful information regarding potential crisis situations or accident hazards.[9]

The practice of preventive medicine involves three steps. First, the physician must assess the long term risks to which a patient is subject. Second, one must plan preventive measures focused on the reduction of these risks. Third, one must organize a clinical record on each patient, so that one can monitor the progress of the preventive plan.[10]

Therapy

The family physician should be capable of handling the complete needs of most patients. Yet one must also observe the limitations, and avoid spending inordinate amounts of time with patients whose problems are either too simple or too complex. Yet, the family physician does often engage in emergency care, and sometimes in surgery. At the very least, he/she is the one who determines the need for surgery and carries the bulk of the pre-operative and post-operative care.[11]

The family physician's mere presence can produce improvement. Consequently, one must never appear aloof, casual, hurried, or even give a hint of avoidance. Yet one must take care to keep compassion in perspective, and not allow oneself to identify with the patient on too personal a level.[12]

In order to provide this quality care, the family physician needs to conduct repetitive checkups and keep good written records. One tool for monitoring patient status is the flow chart, which records, in adjacent columns, all data pertaining to a specific problem. Here the physician records the date, the progression of an illness, medications used, possible complications, other illnesses which could adversely affect the primary condition, the patient's understanding of the disease, and compliance with instructions. A companion tool to the flow chart is the problem list, recording any problem, date first observed, and either date resolved or date and name of next stage or occurrence.[13]

Rehabilitation

The family physician is responsible, after an illness, for preserving as much functioning ability as possible. This rehabilitation involves physical, mental, emotional, financial, social and spiritual readjustments. The family physician needs to give attention not only to medical needs, but also to development of hobbies, homemaking skills, and job rehabilitation. One must encourage increasing independence on the part of the patient and adjustment on the part of the family. Consequently, it is important

125

to provide the family with any instructions and even include them in the rehabilitative planning.[14]

Referral

After the family physician makes an accurate appraisal of the health care problem, he/she may recommend seeing a specialist. In this act of referral, it is the responsibility of the family physician to discuss fees and clarify relationships and responsibilities among all parties.[15] In addition, one must interpret to the patient, explaining the nature of the illness, the implications of treatment, and the effect of both upon the patient's life. Finally, one should follow-up to ensure that the patient receives maximum benefit from the referral.[16]

Coordinating Functions

In addition to coordinating the treatment given by specialists, the family physician can serve as captain of a team of allied health personnel working under him/her. One ought to understand the training and skills of these persons, and know how they can contribute to the care of the patient. One must become comfortable with delegation of responsibility, understanding that he/she is not the only one capable of performing certain functions or seeing certain patients.[17]

Normally, these allied health personnel include task oriented specialists, such as physical therapists and dieticians, as well as professional generalists. Among the latter one usually finds social workers, nurses, physicians' assistants and family health workers. The functions they perform include history taking, performing laboratory tests and basic examinations, some diagnosis and therapy, counseling, health education, and contacting outside resources. The social worker adds to family practice a unique ability to address the social and emotional aspects of health care. The nurse brings a special concern for the patient, a caring and comforting orientation. The physician's assistant is more oriented toward the physician, organizing data on each patient and presenting it to him/her before the patient leaves. The family health worker's special contribution is the building of bridges between family, health care team, and specialists, increasing each one's understanding of the others.[18]

Community Functions

The family physician's leadership is crucial for improving the quantity and quality of the other health resources and services within the community. One needs to inform and involve oneself in the planning of hospital facilities, community clinics, and other health resources. The physician's voice carries much influence in the guidance of public opinion on health and environmental issues.[19]

Adapting The Model

Similarities And Differences

Similarities

The pastor has much in common with the family physician. Both are second level helping professions, initial resource people after the non-professional "caretaker."[20] Both are specialists in breadth who focus attention on family units and concentrate on health or growth. In each case, the care needs to be both comprehensive and continuous. In addition, diagnostic, preventive, and therapeutic procedures are all a part of pastoral care, though they are not as easily distinguishable from one another as in health care. The Biblical material from chapter 2 presents the need for shepherds to know and observe (diagnose) the flock before they can reach out to care for them. Furthermore, the initial reaching out has to be positive and upbuilding (preventive care) in order to gain the rapport necessary to address any problems or pathologies (therapeutic care). Finally, in accord with both Biblical material and the family physician model, the shepherd must act as coordinator, encouraging the flock, especially the lay leadership, to be this kind of support for one another. Consequently, the examination of both lay and pastoral care should include the four phases of diagnosis, prevention, therapy, and coordination.

Differences

The family physician model emphasizes relationships, within the health team and between physician and patient/family. This sufficiently satisfies the basic need for a sense of community within health care. However, the church is able to develop an even greater sense of community. In the church, those served and the helping team are often the same, the people of the congregation. This dual role entails greater lay participation in all phases of care and enhances comprehensive and continuous care. It also gives the church leader a multi-faceted relationship with the parishioners, the "one served" and the "fellow servant." Consequently the setting for care is usually less formal than the physician's office.

The most significant difference is the church's need to focus on providing positive growth, rather than alleviating problems and pathologies. The family physician model, despite its purported non-disease orientation, continues to be too problem-centered in practice. The purpose of preventive medicine is still stated in terms of campaigning against disease. In the church the ministry of preventive care must emphasize the building of spiritual health. Any diagnostic techniques must train the eye to look for signs of health as well as pathology. Even in therapeutic care, by definition pathological in focus, the church leader should find ways to promote growth, rather than merely relieve problems.

Spiritual Diagnosis

The shepherding task of knowing and observing is an active one, requiring great initiative on the part of the church leader. The first responsibility is to gather the flock, to seek out each individual, discovering areas of growth as well as symptoms of problems, talents and abilities as well as needs. One should come to know each one well enough to identify that person's unique strengths and weaknesses, in effect, to call him or her by name. Although each person does have his/her own unique blend of characteristics, it is helpful, in the naming process, to group together or classify parishioners. Such a classification can then assist one to establish priorities for further care. Possible categories can include: church leaders (officers plus those responsible for specific programs), those especially open to learning and growing, those undergoing crisis (emergencies like sickness, accidents and bereavements, or developmental crises like marriage and retirement), shut-ins, those needing counseling, the elderly, other active members, inactive members, friends and visitors of the church.

The Assessment

Most persons, when they first speak to a church leader do not bring a specific concern; they come simply desiring to be cared for and helped to grow. This makes it difficult for both pastor and laity to make any kind of formal assessment. Yet the effective caretaker will still attempt to identify the areas of growth or difficulty as specifically as possible and interpret the meaning and implications for both oneself and the other person.

The primary tool will simply be conversation, a less formal process than the family physician's initial interview. Yet, like the family physician, the church caretaker needs to begin with a person where he/she is, seeking to understand any feelings, concerns, problems, behaviors, and the situations which produced them. One seeks to discover any significant experiences, needs and opinions regarding such things as family, education, vocation, and religion. In all this, care for the individual must supercede mere acquisition of information. The exact approach should depend on the individual's stage of life, frame of reference, and degree of self-directedness. Generally one does more listening than talking, asks open ended questions, and temporarily suspends judgments.

The Record

It is wise, especially for the pastor, to record visits and counseling sessions, including date and location, carefully noting any promises made to individual or family. In addition, one may keep a separate file for each household, beginning such a record with an historical data sheet (see Fig. 1). Following this, one can comprise, for each household, a list of present areas of growth, problem, risk or celebration (see Fig. 2). Finally, one may occasionally wish to write verbatim or critical incident reports, particularly in times of controversy, confusion, and anxiety, in order to enhance his/her understanding of the person. Most of these records must remain confidential. Only the historical data sheet should be accessible even to office personnel.

Figure 1
Historical Data Sheet

Family and Health Information

    Names   Relationship in Family   Decade Born In

    Names of Physicians and Other Health Care
    Professionals

Educational and Vocational Information

    Degrees/Certificates/Licenses

    Jobs Held

    Retirement

Religious Information

    Religious Background

    Baptisms or Dedications

    Church Membership

    Participation in the Church

        Church Offices Held

        Administrative/Committee Work

        Special Church Programs

        Study and Fellowship Groups

        Mission Projects

        Ministry to Individuals

Information on Secular Activities

    Secular Organizations to Which Belong (Note
    Leadership Positions)

    Other Community or Civic Involvements

    Special Interests/Hobbies

Figure 2
GROWTH POTENTIAL CHART
(Areas of Growth, Problem, Risk, Celebration)

Date	Self-Understanding	Date	Health	Date	Family	Date	Education/ Vocation	Date	Social Relationships/ Ministry to Others	Date	Faith/ Church Life

Preventive care is a greater part of a church leader's function than that of the family physician. The pastor, especially, is in a unique position, and has a special responsibility, to minister to "healthy" persons. Unlike most other professionals, one has regular access to any home or office, and informal contact at church functions. Most pastor-parishioner relationships never extend beyond preventive care; for those which do, this is still the foundation for further care.

The main purpose of ecclesiastical, as distinct from medical, preventive care is more than averting the occurrence, or delaying the progression, of spiritual disease. It is the attempt to facilitate growth in devotion and service to Christ by developing an ongoing relationship with the person. By identifying with parishioners through listening, questioning, and clarifying, the church leader can encourage them to trust him or her. We can sum up this preventive responsibility in a two-fold task, feeding and guiding (to use Biblical categories), or sustaining and guiding (to use the categories of pastoral care historians, Clebsch and Jaekle).[21] The church leader must sustain and guide the flock through the use of prayer, communion, Scripture reading, or other religious resources, that they might attain mature relationships with God, others, and themselves.

Sustaining

Sustaining care implies not only feeding and nourishing, but also the Biblical images of protecting, warning, and defending the flock. The church leader must help people to recognize misconceptions of the Christian faith which threaten to distort their Christian lives. One must also provide support and comfort for any distressed persons, especially shut-ins and those in the midst of crisis.

Yet the primary task of sustaining care is the strengthening, inspiring, and encouraging of the people. To adequately feed the flock, one needs to stimulate and energize the parishioner so that self-confidence, self-discipline, and competence increase to the greatest degree possible. Primarily this involves bringing a word of hope and encouragement, stated in a way which the parishioner can hear, and which realistically takes into account any of his or her concerns. Occasionally it may mean confronting someone in order that they may come to see with a new and fresh perspective. One's very presence carries much significance in the process of building up the people. Consequently, one must be faithful in regular visitation, yet taking care not to create an over-dependence on oneself by overvisiting. When one does visit, how much or what one says may be of less importance than how much and how well one listens.

Guiding

Guidance is the attempt to help the parishioner adjust to new circumstances or make decisions; it is usually short-term. Church membership, marriage, birth, death, vocation, or education are some of the new circumstances in which people seek better under-standing and adjustment. Prior to church membership and marriage, the church leader should offer guidance through a series of classes or counseling sessions, respectively. In addition to providing content and direction through formal instruction, one needs to give personal application through listening and ques-tioning appropriately. In other circumstances, such as ministry to a family at times of birth or death, one usually gives a less structured form of guidance. Prior to the baptism, dedication, or funeral, one normally spends informal times with the family, lis-tening and clarifying, accompanied by a similar follow-up visit. Other new circumstances, such as education or job, require even less structure. One needs to be sensitive at these times to pick up an individual's desire to talk. Finally, one should include, in each person's file, records of any bap-tisms or dedications, funerals, confirmations, or premarital counseling sessions.

To guide a person in making decisions the church leader should not provide ready-made directives. Instead, one must first listen, occasionally question, and check to make sure one understands the issue. Then one must help the individual to see the alter-natives, perceive the advantages and disadvantages of each, ascertain, and act on, his or her basic desires in the light of these insights. By doing this one encourages the person's sense of responsibility to make his or her own decisions.

133

Although both laity and other professionals have important roles in therapeutic care, the pastor's constant availability and unhurried presence are essential whenever a critical problem arises for any parishioner. In addition to the listening, questioning, and clarifying emphases of preventive care, therapeutic care requires more intervention and confrontation in order to enable the parishioner to take some appropriate action. Depending on the individual parishioner, and the exact circumstances, the church caretaker may utilize the resources of Scripture, communion and prayer as therapeutic tools.

When the church leader lacks either sufficient training, resources, time, or emotional distance, one should refer, or introduce, the parishioner to another helping person for purpose of treatment and/or growth. Yet one must neither abandon the individual nor confuse the caretaker task with that of the specialist, even if the latter is a form of pastoral ministry such as pastoral counseling. Instead, the church leader performs a unique, supportive function during this period, while also assuming primary responsibility for "pre-specialist" and "post-specialist," or rehabilitative, care. When one determines the need for referral, one may suggest this to the parishioner, informing him or her of the nature and consequences of the services recommended, giving names, locations and costs of specific individuals or agencies. Yet one should allow the parishioner to initiate the contact. In the event of a delay in obtaining specialized help, one needs to provide ongoing care and perhaps emergency counseling. During the period of referral one must help establish confidence in the specialist, and facilitate understanding between all parties. After the referral period one may need to provide stability and security for a parishioner with "re-entry" needs.

The exact nature of therapeutic care depends on many factors, including family, individual frame of reference, age, education, sex, degree of church involvement, and race, ethnicity or sub-culture. We can, however, categorize this care into two basic tasks, correcting or restoring the soul and healing (to use Biblical descriptions), or reconciling and healing (to draw upon the history of pastoral care).[22]

Reconciling

Reconciling care attempts to re-establish relationships with God and with men and women. The two ancient modes of providing this care, confession and church discipline, are still the primary tools, though modified in practice. When the church leader functions in the role of confessor, it is incumbent on one to remember the reconciling nature of this task. The caretaker's primary concern is with relationships, not sins. Consequently, one should help the parishioner to confess to the appropriate party. The parishioner needs to experience the forgiveness of the one wronged, not just the absolution of the church leader.

The family physician imparts a certain kind of discipline to the patient through the prescribing of medication, diet, exercise, and other measures. Likewise, the church, as a covenant community, based on mutually accepted agreements, should set out disciplines which become standards for membership. Some of these disciplines should be concrete and specific, such as regular exercise of prayer, Scripture reading, worship and tithing. Others may refer generally to one's commitment to God, one's church, and the individual members. However, unlike the medical profession, the church must concern itself, not only with ordered responses to set standards, but with disciplinary measures taken when a person violates these standards. First, the church leader needs to ensure that the person understands that there has been a breach of agreement. Second, a group from the church might follow-up the initial contact, in the pattern of Matt. 18:15f. Finally, it sometimes becomes necessary to recommend the removal of the person from the membership rolls, or some lesser restriction. Yet the caretaker must invariably keep in mind the reconciling purpose of this task. The aim is always to produce repentance, to place people in a situation where they can re-establish good relationships, to make them desire the fellowship they are now missing. This task requires a tender, yet firm, kind of care.

Healing

The healing ministry fosters the continual development of the whole person (mind, body, emotion, spirit). Yet it is distinct from the personal growth focus of preventive care. It involves helping one to leave behind all "false selves" and affirm one's "true self."

135

The link between this ministry and that of reconciling is enormous. The latter is a prerequisite for
the former. The honesty of a penitent heart, coupled
with the hope of a forgiven and forgiving heart, is
essential to the development of both self-acceptance
and the acceptance of others, the building blocks of
emotional, spiritual, and often physical, healing.
Consequently, the pastoral, or lay, healer must be a
person of prayer and penitence on a deeply personal
level, as well as a person of compassion and confrontation on an interpersonal level.

Throughout church history this ministry has included prayer, laying on of hands, anointing, holy
communion, exorcism, and more recently, counseling.
The older disciplines are all part of the ancient
tradition of spiritual direction.[23] There is much
overlap between spiritual direction and counseling.
The differences are ones of emphasis, with the former
focusing on one's relationship with God and the latter
focusing on one's relationship with oneself.

Spiritual direction and counseling are more controlled contexts than other forms of care, with
successive appointments which should be unhurried,
private, and uninterrupted. Still, they are less
structured than the physician's care, necessitating
more frequent redefinition and clarification. In most
cases it is unrealistic for the church leader to
engage in anything beyond short-term involvement.

Any counseling or spiritual direction must be
individually tailored. However, the process generally
follows a certain modus operandi. The first step is
to develop the trust of the person. Second, one must
begin to define the relationship, familiarizing oneself with the person's history, and other professional
contacts, and outline areas of mutual responsibility.
Third, the counselor needs to help the person face
oneself by carefully exploring and listening for the
underlying issues and sometimes confronting the person. Likewise, the spiritual director needs to help
the person to face God by carefully discerning the
state of one's spirit and encouraging an encounter
with God in which one experiences the presence of
Christ in the midst of past and present hurts or
future anxieties. This should include actual prayer,
as well as talk about one's relationship with God.
Fourth, the caretaker should conclude each session
with a summary or interpretation. One should point
out areas of both progress and future consideration,

issues which the person can work on alone and in consultation. Fifth, one may wish to keep a "flow chart" in the person's file, recording, in sequence, all the data pertaining to one particular concern. (See Fig. 3) Finally, when one will no longer see the person in this capacity, one must properly terminate the relationship.

Coordinating the Care

Care is not solely the calling of the pastor. He or she has the assistance of other professionals as well as church laity. Along with this comes the responsibility to coordinate the care administered by the variety of persons. To single-handedly provide comprehensive and continuous care, as described above, for the entire congregation would be overbearing and impossible. To attempt this kind of care for more than a handful of people is to forget the Biblical pattern of shepherding, which includes building a caring community. It also ignores the lesson of medieval church history when the clergy claimed sole access to God and thereby to the ministry of care in God's name. If the pastor spends most of the time with the healthy, one can motivate and train them to minister more deeply to the rest of the congregation than one could by oneself.

Lay Responsibilities

The church may well pattern its system of shared responsibilities for caring after the family physician's allied health team. The composition and function of this team varies according to the type, size, and location of the church; the training, experience, and interests of individuals; and the needs of both church and community. Yet, normally, the deacons, elders, or other lay leadership could become the "pastor's (physician's) assistants." Lay callers and leaders of fellowship groups like Bible studies, women's groups, prayer groups, and mission groups could become a core of "parish (family) health workers."

The pastor needs "parish health workers," or under-shepherds, to act as primary contact persons on behalf of the church, administering continuous care

Figure 3
HEALING FLOW CHART

Name(s)	Date	Type of Session	Presenting Problem	Main Issues/Progress Made in Understanding or Behavior/ Remaining Issues	Referrals

for specific individuals. In this capacity they may become informal history takers and diagnosticians for a pastor who wishes to reach all those who need professional attention. The undershepherds can lead people with greater needs to the pastor and deacons. Yet, with training, they can also provide much preventive care and reach out to discover and meet many needs. Most should be somewhat capable of sustaining and praying for persons under their care; some are capable of rendering guidance. In addition, these undershepherds may be able to provide varying degrees of therapeutic care. Their mere presence is crucial in the midst of crisis. Some are able to assist constructively in the reconciliation process. A few, through their profession or by volunteering in a social agency, may have the necessary information and/or position to refer someone to a needed specialist. A very few may have the gifts or spiritual direction and counseling.

The "pastor's assistants," deacons or other lay leadership, may be called upon to do anything a pastor does, depending on their interests or abilities and the expectations of the church. Certainly they should be able to perform the ministries of the undershepherds and to handle some referrals from them. They share equally with the pastor the task of including confined persons in the life and care of the church. Moreover, they have a special responsibility to minister to the pastor. Finally, they must assist in the coordination of any effective church shepherding program.

Pastoral Responsibilities

The pastor should set an example of caring for the laity in the same way Jesus did for his disciples. Initially, while preparing his "counselors-in-training," Jesus met most of the needs presented to him. Likewise, the pastor, at first, ought to do more visiting himself. Yet one should do so on the basis of need, taking into consideration parishioner expectations. Above all the pastor must become the primary contact person for the lay leadership and undershepherds, helping them to grow and develop as persons in Christ, providing both preventive and therapeutic care, and modeling for them continuity of care. This involves taking a great deal of initiative in relation to them, while at the same time empowering them to be shepherds. It also involves knowing them well enough to sensitively link their capabilities with parishioners' needs.

The pastor is ultimately responsible for developing and overseeing the church's comprehensive care program, a task simplified by extensive contact with both the needy and the potential helping person. To develop such a program, the pastor should begin by soliciting the support of the lay leadership, explaining the value, asking for input, suggesting possible involvements, and accepting their level of participation. Second, the pastor, and any supportive lay leadership, may need to initiate, or revitalize, fellowship groups and lay callers. Third, the pastor may offer training in the care of persons. Once underway, the structure of this program could resemble the oversight of small groups, described in chapter 5, where the pastor trains and leads a group of group leaders. The topics for the training program ought to be easily recognizable as areas of concern. In this continuous training and support, undershepherds and deacons could share, encourage, and exchange constructive criticism with one another.

Summary

The church needs a shepherding program in which pastor and laity work together to provide both preventive and therapeutic care. In a well-established program the laity can do much of the need identification, diagnosis and preventive care, and some therapeutic care. The pastor should spend more time than the laity in therapeutic care, though not forgetting to develop relationships of good rapport through diagnosis and prevention.

The task of diagnosis involves seeking out and classifying the persons in the congregation. Pastor and laity must assess each person's areas of growth or difficulty. The pastor is wise to keep some records of this information on each household. Preventive care encompasses the greatest amount of time for both pastor and laity. The aim of this ministry to healthy persons is to facilitate growth in service to Christ. Two types of preventive care are necessary, sustaining and guiding. Sustaining is the task of protecting, warning and defending the flock, as well as feeding, nourishing, strengthening, and encouraging the congregation. Guiding is the task of assisting someone to adjust to new circumstances or make decisions.

Therapeutic care is more problem-centered than preventive care, yet, even here, the church leader must concern oneself with the development of spiritual health. The two-fold task of therapeutic care is reconciling and healing. The former involves the encouragement of confession and the administration of church discipline; the latter involves spiritual direction and counseling. When the caretaker becomes aware of reaching the limitations of one's ability to assist someone, he or she must be willing to, and know how to, refer the individual to another helping person. Finally, the pastor must develop and oversee this program of care, training and encouraging the lay leadership and undershepherds. By providing continual care for them and their families, one can model the kind of care which they can provide for the rest of the church.

1. Advisory Manual prepared by the Committee On Medical Economics of the American Academy of General Practice, Raymond Kahn, Chairman, Organization and Management of Family Practice (Kansas City, Missouri: American Academy of General Practice, 1968), pp. 3, 5 and 9.

2. Ibid., pp. 11-12.

3. Ibid., p. 3.

4. Report of the Ad Hoc Committee on Education for Family Practice of the Council on Medical Education, American Medical Association, William Willard, Chairman, Meeting the Challenge of Family Practice (Chicago: Council on Medical Education, American Medical Association, 1966), p. 8.

5. Ibid., p. 7.

6. Robert Roek and C. Robert Baisden, "Health Screening: Early Detection of Disease," in Family Practice, ed. by Howard Conn, Robert Rakel, and Thomas Johnson (Philadelphia: W.B. Saunders Co., 1973), pp. 83-85.

7. Robert Froelich and Jack Verby, "Interviewing Techniques," in Family Practice, ed. by Howard Conn, Robert Rakel, and Thomas Johnson (Philadelphia: W.B. Saunders Co., 1973), pp. 231-237.

8. Joseph Stokes III and L. J. Schneiderman, "The Clinical Practice of Preventive Medicine," in Family Practice, ed. by Howard Conn, Robert Rakel, and Thomas Johnson (Philadelphia: W.B. Saunders Co., 1973), p. 57.

9. Organization and Management of Family Practice, pp. 12-13.

10. Theodore Phillips, "The Preventive Attitude," in Family Practice, ed. by Howard Conn, Robert Rakel, and Thomas Johnson (Philadelphia: W.B. Saunders Co., 1973), p. 72.

11. _Organization and Management of Family Practice_, pp. 13-15.

12. Tennyson Williams and J. B. Corley, "The Management of Chronic Illness," in _Family Practice_, ed. by Howard Conn, Robert Rakel, and Thomas Johnson (Philadelphia: W.B. Saunders Co., 1973), p. 112.

13. _Ibid._, pp. 112-117.

14. J. Blair Pace, "Rehabilitation," in _Family Practice_, ed. by Howard Conn, Robert Rakel, and Thomas Johnson (Philadelphia: W.B. Saunders Co., 1973), pp. 175-181.

15. _Organization and Management of Family Practice_, p. 16.

16. _Meeting the Challenge of Family Practice_, p. 9.

17. _Ibid._, pp. 7-10.

18. Derek Peske, Libby Tanner, and Thomas Aschenbrener, "The Allied Health Professions," in _Family Practice_, ed. by Howard Conn, Robert Rakel, and Thomas Johnson (Philadelphia: W.B. Saunders Co., 1973), pp. 130-136; and

Len Hughes Andrus and John P. Geyman, "Managing the Health Care Team," in _Family Practice_, ed. by Howard Conn, Robert Rakel, and Thomas Johnson (Philadelphia: W.B. Saunders Co., 1973), pp. 141-144.

19. Hiram Curry and Silas Grant, "Role of the Family Physician," in _Family Practice_, ed. by Howard Conn, Robert Rakel, and Thomas Johnson (Philadelphia: W.B. Saunders Co., 1973), p. 48.

20. Thomas Klink, _Depth Perspectives In Pastoral Work_, Successful Pastoral Counseling Series (Philadelphia: Fortress Press, 1969), pp. 58-59.

21. William A. Clebsch and Charles R. Jaekle, _Pastoral Care In Historical Perspective_ (Englewood Cliffs, New Jersey: Prentice-Hall, Inc., 1964), pp. 8-9.

22. _Ibid_.

23. Kenneth Leech, _Soul Friend: The Practice of Christian Spirituality_ (San Francisco: Harper and Row, Publishers, 1977), pp. 121-134.

CHAPTER VIII

AUTHORITY

Throughout this book, I have addressed various issues of authority. In Part I, I examined the questions of basis, source and recipient of authority, and looked at the function of eldership, the function of being the "authority figure," the wise old man who represented God to the people and the people to God. In Part II, I have dealt, to some extent, with authority issues as they relate to each of the models examined thus far. However, I have not yet developed a model which deals primarily with the function of "authority figure" or elder. The purpose of this chapter is to develop such a model through the examination of a secular profession which parallels the Biblical concept of eldership. I will first ask what responsibilities are required to establish this person's authority. Then I will investigate the influence of official and charismatic authority, the various sources of authority, and both shared and unique aspects of authority, all on the nature and performance of these requisite responsibilities.

In choosing a secular model I think first of government, often referred to as, "The Authorities." The Old Testament reinforces this selection with its emphasis on the governmental tasks of an elder, a term even equated with alderman.[1] Moreover, we often hear city aldermen, or councilors, referred to as "The City Fathers," with all the patriarchal overtones. The city councilor model is a good example of multiple leadership. Yet, to parallel the Biblical pattern, we must look to the presiding officer of the council, historically the major.[2] Given the parallel between this model and the Biblical norms for pastoral authority, as well as the common need within both governmental and ecclesiastical bodies to develop a sense of community, the mayor becomes the good choice.

Before proceeding, we must clarify which mayoral model we are using. Two types of city government predominate today in the United States, mayor-council and council-manager. Most municipalities utilize a combination of the "weak mayor" and "strong mayor" plans within the mayor-council form. Such a government functions by creating a balance between the powers of mayor and council. Council-manager government, the

most recent and fastest growing model, uses a professional chief administrator. The mayor relinquishes
most executive functions to this city manager, retain-
ing, along with the councilors, authority or power
over him or her.[3] The ideal model would be a combination of these two. Like a mayor-council government it would hold a direct, popular election for a
mayor who would retain executive function, so important to the pastoral role. Yet it would be one in
which the mayor is part of, and presides over, the
council, as in council-manager government. We find
such a model in the "modified weak mayor plan" of the
State of Wisconsin.[4]

The Mayor In Municipal Government

Anything the mayor does affects one's authentica-
tion as an authority figure, yet some actions are
especially important. One's functions as ceremonial
representative are those most unique and central to
the role, as seen by the sole retention of them in
council-manager government.[5]

Ceremonial Representative Responsibilities

The mayor is the living symbol of the city, representing and reflecting its spirit.[6] Consequently, one must adopt a public image, adjusting to
the "givens" and molding one's unique expression of
the role. Accepting the "givens" includes coming to
terms with the electorate's high expectations. Often
these expectations can be overwhelming, carrying implications of omnipresence, omnipotence, and omni-
science.[7] The mayor must allow constituents to hold
these lofty views of him or her, yet recognize, for
oneself, any limitations and failures. In short, one
needs to avoid both the abdication and arrogance of
authority.

Representing The City To Itself

The mayor first represents the city to itself.
According to Henry Maier, mayor of Milwaukee,[8] the
mayor must make regular contact with the people, going
where the people are, while still respecting the existence of a "special distance" because one is not an
ordinary person. Second, the public expects the mayor
to attend community functions and to endorse worthy

causes. Third, the mayor serves as a master of ceremonies who greets celebrities, reviews parades, and
presides over openings. Fourth, the mayor is a source
of news and general spokesperson for the city. Fifth,
mayors are responsible for devising a "definite plan
of reporting to citizens on municipal affairs" through
annual and special reports. Sixth, the mayor must
sign many official city papers, each having the potential for a ceremony surrounding the signing.

Representing The City To Outside
Governmental And Private Entities

The mayor is also a primary municipal representative to other entities, both government and private.
In this context the mayor becomes a lobbyist and negotiator. In addition to affecting the municipal policy
of influential governments, the mayor often must arbi-
trate industrial disputes whenever they affect the
general welfare of the city. One also meets with representatives of business firms considering locating
in the municipality. To lobby most effectively, the
mayor should work to build consensus within the state
municipal league and the United States Conference of
Mayors. As a representative of the city to these organizations, one can foster coordination and cooperation between cities, with state and federal governments, and with the private sector. As the city's
most visible representative, the mayor also becomes
the one to whom these outside groups look to coordinate and implement their concerns and mediate any
disagreements.[9]

Influence on the Exercise of Authority

Personal Charismata

The mayor's personal interests, style, and capabilities must affect the exact nature of one's responsibilities and performance. To avoid putting one's
unique stamp on the office through the exercise of
one's unique charismata, is to court failure.[10] The
only pertinent question is how much can personal factors legitimately alter requisite responsibilities and
suggest supplementary activities.

The mayor, in one's official capacity, can specialize in a few responsibilities, developing one's
own style and relegating other activities to one's
staff. One way to emphasize personal interests is by

147

serving, as a council member, on particular council committees, which comprise a major part of the councilor's (mayor's) work.[11] Consequently, subject to council approval, the mayor can choose areas of specialty, such as finances or public health. Wisconsin even allows the mayor to chair council committees, represent the council on boards and commissions, and function in other official, non-mayoral positions, like state assemblyman or utility commissioner, provided these do not interfere with one's performance of requisite responsibilities.[12] Non-officially, the mayor can join or initiate community organizations or services of interest to her or him, adding the prestige of one's office to the endeavor.

Finally, to specify the effects of personal variables on performance, I point to the book, Mayors In Action: Five Approaches To Urban Governance, by John Kotter and Paul Lawrence. They delineate five types or styles (ceremonial, caretaker, personality/ individualist, the executive, and program entrepreneur). Each, with its own set of skills, encourages a specific approach to agenda setting, network building, and task accomplishment.[13] The ceremonial mayor takes an individual approach to task accomplishment. The executive mayor is discrete in network development. The progressive entrepreneurial mayor firmly directs agenda setting. These are just a few of the variables of performance based on mayoral style.

Accountability

The mayor is clearly accountable primarily to the electorate. They can assert approval or disapproval through compulsory referenda, regular and recall elections, or the request for a council vote. In addition, the mayor must satisfy the written law--state constitution, statutes, special legislation, and city charter. Any violator is subject to removal by the court.[14] Finally, the mayor must prove satisfactory to individuals within state government, like the circuit judge in Wisconsin,[15] who have power of removal for just cause.

Accountability to state law and officials provides incentive to perform well one's obligations as municipal representative to the state, especially in interpreting, preserving, and enforcing the law. The state gives mayor and council primary responsibility to apply the law to the specific municipality by

148

granting them power to enact ordinances, essentially clarifications of state law.[16] Yet, though account-ability to the state has some influence, ultimate ac-countability still rests with the people, since state officials also answer to the electorate.

The predominance of community accountability in-fluences the mayor to please the electorate. Thus, the wise mayor seldom issues ultimatums and carefully exercises the veto, not assuming one is to prevail. Instead, the mayor must carefully gauge, respond to, and shape public opinion.[17]

Coadjutant Relationships

As previously stated, the mayor has unique au-thority as presiding officer of the council, cere-monial head of the electorate, and representative of the community to outsiders. Yet there is often shared authority with the council in legislative, adminis-trative, and judicial matters. Some states grant the mayor full voting rights in the council.[18] Others remove the mayor's distinctiveness by denying veto power.[19] Nevertheless, because the mayor is a fig-urehead, people perceive him or her as having more legislative and administrative pull, sometimes giving one, in fact, more of such power. Consequently, we can say that the mayor has a coadjutant relationship with the city councilors, one in which there is mutual assistance or cooperation, yet in which one person is "primus inter pares," first among equals.

Here, we are interested in the effect of this relationship on the mayor's responsibilities and per-formance. The principal context for the unique aspect of the authority is one's function as presiding offi-cer of the council. In this capacity, the mayor must direct the council toward decisions by clarifying ob-jectives and learning to lead meetings quickly and in an orderly fashion. Yet one must not sacrifice tact, respect, or impartiality.[20]

The shared aspect of the authority involves learning to function corporately in supportive and cooperative ways. One must avoid attacking others, defending oneself, or calling for public support when one differs from a majority of the council, unless the cause is very popular. In addition one needs to know the sentiment of council subgroups, avoid predeter-mined conclusions, keep discussion within the group more than with individuals, look for opportunities to advance the goals of others, and ask for their advice and help.[21]

Adapting The Model

Similarities and Differences

Similarities

The pastor, like the mayor, is a symbolic figure. Lay leadership, like the city council, also serves this symbolic function. Consequently, the church leader needs to adopt a public image by fulfilling many similar functions. The pastor, especially, must serve as a representative to the local church as well as the wider church and secular community. Finally, one's personal charismata, communal accountability, and relationships with the lay leadership must all be taken into account in assessing one's role and authority.

The major concerns I will address regarding authority, then, are the same as those examined in the mayoral model. What does the official nature of one's position entail as an authority figure, and how does it affect how one does it? How do one's personal charismata (as expressed in interests, style, and capabilities) influence one's status as authority figure and one's exercise of that authority? To what extent should one's accountability to the various sources of authority (church community, various individuals, and the Scriptures) affect one's conceptions and use of authority? What is the influence, on responsibilities and performance, of the coadjutant nature of the pastor's relationships with lay leaders (relationships in which the pastor is first among equals, leader of leaders)?

Differences

Pastor and lay leadership differ from mayor and council in that they represent more than just the church community that they lead. Even more significantly, the pastor, in particular, is a representative of God to the people. Since the church leader reminds people of God and of the character of God -- grace, judgment, and call to obedience -- one must attempt to reflect the character of God in one's life. One's authority needs to be undergirded by personal obedience. Yet this obedience must grow out of grace rather than law. Government relies on legal constraint and its authority figures become an embodiment of this law. The church relies on inner transformation and its authority figures are to be an embodiment of this grace. The church leaders' true call to obedience springs from freedom rather than restraint. It grows out of a sense of gratitude rather than compulsion.

The introduction of God as ultimate authority figure, with all its ramifications, should help restrain any tendency to dominate the flock. The church leader must remember that the foundation for one's authority, as portrayed in Scripture, is service (διάκονος). Even more than the mayor, the pastor ceases to be effective when structure or position, power or prestige, becomes the primary focus.

Yet, the church leader cannot abdicate authority either. The fact that one represents God affects the way the laity relates to the pastor. One consequence of this function is the laity's tendency to hide their real selves. The pastor must understand and accept the need for this "special distance." A second consequence is lay persons' tendency to hold God, and therefore God's representative, accountable for the frustrations in their lives. A third result is the high expectations placed on the pastor. It is one thing to represent a city, another to represent God. It is especially important to understand and accept the frustrations and unrealistic expectations of lay persons who want the pastor to be both human and superhuman. At the same time, the pastor must avoid any arrogance of authority by recognizing one's own fallibility. This may mean sharing one's own problems and weaknesses with lay people. But, when one does this, it is important to select lay persons who are able to handle the relationship on these terms and to clarify the purpose of the conversation. To live out this balance between abdication and arrogance, it is critical that one take periodic time for rest and re-examination.

The Church Leader As Ceremonial Representative

Although faithful performance of the other leadership functions -- administration, teaching, and care -- is essential to the development of authority, the ceremonial representative responsibilities are especially important. They are uniquely tied to the

151

conception and use of authority, as they are not part of any other church leadership function. Consequently these requisite responsibilities deserve more detailed attention.

In addition to being a representative of God to the people, the church leader is a representative of the people to God. Since the function of intercession is an important part of this representational task, I will first examine the church leader as representative to God, then as representative to the local congregation, other ecclesiastical bodies, and secular community.

Representative To God

In fulfillment of ordination vows, the church leader comes before God as intercessor for individuals, the church and the community. Publicly, people expect prayer by "an expert" during illness, bereavement, and other occasions of personal need, even when someone else has prayed the most beautiful of prayers. Public prayer in the church may take place during business meetings and fellowship gatherings, as well as worship or prayer meetings. It is especially important for the pastor to accept the performance of this representative responsibility and to do it with integrity, not simply as a guise for teaching or correcting.

Privately, the church leader must develop a regular devotional life, bringing before God, not only one's own concerns and thanksgiving, but also those of persons whom she or he leads. One should not be afraid to promise to pray for individuals, especially within one's congregation. Yet one must take care not to make more promises than one can keep. To overburden oneself does no service to anyone; it only detracts from joy and faithfulness. A discipline, such as praying for different persons on each day of the week, is a way of regularly bringing before God the needs of a relatively large number of individuals, as well as the ministry of a whole congregation. Such prayer may involve specific requests, but often simply means holding people up to the loving presence of God.

Representative To The Local Congregation

The church leader represents both God and the church (local and universal) to the congregation. This ceremonial representative task requires an image adoption process similar to that of the mayor. As representative of the church, the pastor signs official papers, like marriage licenses, baptism and church membership certificates. One receives requests from people to endorse community or church causes. One must report regularly to the church. One is periodically expected to attend meetings of church organizations and function as a master of ceremonies at social events. In addition, the church leader, as representative of both God and church, needs to be a spokesperson, for he or she is a source of news about the congregation and a source of inspiration from God. Since worship is the principal meeting place, unifier and expression of the life of the church, it is the chief context in which the pastor can develop this image in the minds of the people. Consequently, I will concentrate on examining this aspect of the representative function to the local congregation.

The use of ceremony in worship is more apparent in high church liturgy, but present in all. It consists of actions designed to express or illustrate the words, or rite, of the liturgy. It includes such things as joining hands, use of water in baptism, laying on of hands, passing the peace, and extension of arms during the benediction. By being the primary person to initiate or perform these, the pastor, as representative of the congregation, symbolizes the reality of fellowship, and, as representative of God, symbolizes the granting of cleansing, blessing, and spiritual power.

The mere existence of the ceremonies, however, does not guarantee that proper image adoption has taken place. Appearance, conduct, and self-investment during worship indicate one's degree of image adoption and influence the development of one's image in the minds of the people. One must appear and conduct oneself as an ambassador of Christ, continually in relationship with God. One must put oneself into the worship experience, requiring alertness to the Spirit during both preparation and delivery. One's deportment and attire should reflect dignity and reverence, along with warmth and intimacy. The exact patterns will differ from congregation to congregation, depending on denominational, and local traditions.

In all this, the worship leader, in contrast to the mayor, should not seek to draw attention to oneself. The purpose of worship is the adoration of God, not the adulation of the leader. The latter is primarily a fellow worshiper; only secondarily is one the leader or representative up front.

Representative To Other Ecclesiastical Bodies

The pastor, in particular, functions as a liaison between the congregation and both the denomination and other church and parachurch organizations. This is comparable to the mayor's relationship to state, federal and other municipal and local governments, such as school districts, metropolitan districts, and other cities.

As the local congregation's representative, the pastor has certain obligations to both the local church and the wider church. On behalf of the local church one should, as much as possible, share the needs of the congregation with the area minister, bishop, or district superintendent, as well as fellow pastors, that they might knowledgeably advise and pray for pastor and church. Likewise, one may attempt to gain support for programs which affect one's local congregation. Finally, one should attend (and, when appropriate, recruit lay people to attend) clergy associations, other planning groups for inter-church activities, special workshops or seminars, and meetings of the denominational conference or district.

In spite of this responsibility as liaison, the pastor is not primarily a lobbyist. There is virtual autonomy within ecumenical relationships, as compared with the city's more intricate relationship with other local governments. In addition, in most cases, there is greater autonomy in the relationship between local congregation and denomination than in that between city and state. Since this type of relationship exists, the pastor can initiate positive moves whereby both denomination and wider church can serve the local parish.

On behalf of the denomination and ecumenical organizations, the pastor, like the mayor, is responsible to promote the purposes and programs of the wider church as they apply to one's congregation. The pastor and lay leadership must exemplify a spirit of working together with sister churches, that they might inspire the people to a relationship of love and commitment to the world-wide church.

Representative To Secular Community

Just as the mayor represents the city to non-governmental interests, such as labor and business, the pastor, in particular, represents both church and God to the whole community. In this capacity one may have persons or groups from the community come for help regarding such things as funerals, weddings, financial needs, support for some cause, announcement of a community program, or the need for building facilities. In exercising this responsibility one must remember that anything he or she does, or does not do, reflects on the image of the congregation in the community. Therefore, when desirable, it is wise for the pastor to involve the lay leadership in setting guidelines for these relationships.

In addition, the church leader has responsibility to initiate involvement in the community. One at least needs to inform oneself of social and community concerns. Furthermore, one should strive to develop relationships with those who represent the community, as well as those, who through close association, can enhance one's ministry. This involves meeting these persons and volunteering one's own services and those of one's church (pending congregational approval). Sometimes the pastor, in particular, may have the opportunity to voice an opinion through news releases and attendance at various community meetings.

Besides offering support on behalf of the church to the community, the church leader must carefully, yet resolutely, represent the causes of the church, or of God, before the community. This could mean anything from evangelism to being an advocate of the congregation before the rest of the community. To do this, one must have confidence in the people of the church. Finally, one can also enhance the church's name by publicly and privately commending various persons or groups who have performed a service of benefit to the community.

Influences On the Exercise Of Authority

We must look now at the requisite responsibilities in the light of the basis of authority, the sources of authority, and the shared, yet unique, nature of authority. Consequently, as with the mayor, I will examine the influence of personal charismata, accountability, and coadjutant relationships on the nature and performance of church leadership.

Personal Charismata

The emergence of the local church, as the source of authority to whom the church leader is primarily accountable, places greater emphasis on lay responsibility and ministry. Thus our age might be more tempted to favor charismatic authority, in which case we need to learn from sectarian Reformation groups who lost any sense of official authority and pastoral office. However, due to neglect of personal charismata throughout most of church history, there is more precedent to overcome in the other direction. Consequently, we must emphasize the importance of one's gifts in determining specific leadership role and authority.

Capability, as well as interests and style, should be criteria for determining gifts. As seen in the Biblical pattern of charismatic authority, the level of effective functioning demonstrates the degree of authentic authority. Capability, in turn, comes from having personally experienced what one is relating to others. This authority rests ultimately on an inner confidence based on personal integration of one's own experience. If one clearly applies a certain principle to one's life, or demonstrates a specific knowledge or skill, or invests oneself in a particular action, one naturally acquires authority in that area of life. Though Jesus had the official position of Son of God, it was the exercise of his gifts that made him convincing as an authority.

To allow personal charismata to influence the tasks a church leader does, the church must not expect him or her to be expert in everything, but must permit her or him, like the mayor and councilors, to emphasize requisite responsibilities in which one is gifted, de-emphasize those in which one is not, and add some non-essential activities. One way the church leader can specialize is through church committees, task forces, or mission projects. In addition, one may delegate some responsibilities in which one is not gifted. Finally, one may utilize one's gifts through involvement beyond the local parish, as long as the activity does not interfere with requisite responsibilities.

Differing personal charismata also produce variety in approaches to various tasks. Because church authority is based more on grace than law, there is even more freedom in determining specific approaches to functioning. The main restriction is the servanthood nature of the authority of church leaders. To illustrate the potential variation, I will utilize Samuel Southard's seven styles of pastoral leadership: the pietist, the reflector, the evangelist-moralist, the resource man, the personalist, the pragmatist, and the liturgist. [22] Looking at the various approaches to agenda setting, network building, and task accomplishment, as I did with the mayor, a variety of patterns emerge, based on the presence of personal charismata. In agenda setting the personalist has an individualistic approach compared to the resource man's corporate one. In network building the pragmatist is discrete, approaching each type of person differently, whereas the pietist and the liturgist emphasize a universal approach that reaches everyone. In task accomplishment the reflector adopts a non-directive approach, the evangelist-moralist a directive one.

Accountability

As already noted, the church leader is ultimately accountable to God. Any accountability to human persons or the written Word is but a means for expressing this supreme accountability. Maintaining a balance among the three penultimate sources of authority (not an easy task as seen from history) helps keep this ultimate accountability to God in focus. The pastor must keep in mind that she or he is accountable to individuals within the denominational hierarchy, who initially bestow authority at ordination. Later, accountability to the denominational executive increases the pastor's motivation to involve the local church in denominational activities, developing needed relationships with sister churches. Similarly, a healthy degree of accountability to the Scriptures helps keep both church life and leadership authority tied to Biblical principles. One cannot determine ultimate matters of faith and conduct by either majority rule or pastoral proclamation.

Like the mayor and council, the church leader is primarily accountable to the community, the local congregation. This helps the church leader increase in competence and view one's authority in servanthood terms. It encourages one to entreat and inspire rather than compel and coerce. This does not imply complete accommodation out of a desire for acceptance or prestige. It does not give one the right to ignore the concerns of the minority or distort the gospel in order to please the majority. One's concerns must be Biblically-based, yet acted out in a way that is meaningful to the community within which one works. Furthermore, as a servant, responsible primarily to the local congregation, the church leader cannot merely send the laity out to minister. One must become personally involved and go with them. One cannot see oneself as separate from the church. He or she needs to demonstrate a concern for cohesiveness within the body. Thus the primacy of communal accountability intensifies one's sensitivity to the role of "playing coach."

Communal accountability also forces the pastor, in particular, to come to terms with lay expectations, no matter how superhuman or superspiritualized. Like the mayor, one must accurately gauge, and respond to, these expectations. The precise image adoption process will differ from church to church and the pastor needs to adapt oneself to the particular style of the church one serves. Yet one should always give close attention to any feedback, direct or indirect. Even when lay perspectives would limit and distort one's understanding of ministry, the church leader needs to deal with these expectations, keeping lines of communication open and listening to criticism and opposition. At times, one may, like the mayor, need to set aside one's own goals and ride with the events of the moment. However, the church leader must always be sensitive to the opportunity to shape parishioners' opinions by spelling out one's goals in the context of their concerns and accomplishments.

Coadjutant Relationships

As already noted, the pastor, like the mayor, must share authority with the lay leadership. Even Catholic theologian Hans Kung writes, "Much that can be said of him (the pastor) is true of him, not in the sense that it applies to him alone, but in the sense that it applies to him especially."[23] If the pastor, alone, performs too many functions, there is great temptation to see him or her as the only possible channel of grace. Ideally, the lay leadership should be able to do anything that the pastor does, much as the coadjutor bishop assists the bishop in charge at a diocese. For example, lay coadjutors, or assistants, should be able to lead in worship, and even preside over celebration of the Lord's Supper, just as a city councilor may fill in for, or accompany, the mayor at a ceremonial function. Kung asserts that the notion of the ordained person possessing "a sacral-judicial <u>potestas</u> that qualifies him alone to administer the Eucharist and all other sacraments. . . . The time for that sort of monopoly of divine grace has passed, in great matters and in small." He concludes, "All Christians are empowered to carry out baptism and the Eucharist . . ." [24] At the very least, the church ought to expect its lay leadership to participate in all ritualistic activity, in order to give visibility to their ministry and establish their authority. This includes taking part in baptisms, weddings, funerals, and the bringing of worship or communion to confined persons. This does not mean that every believer should do anything. Pastor and church must discern gifts for leading the congregation in ceremony and ritual. Willingness is only one criterion; spiritual fitness and capability are also important.

The pastor does have a special symbolic role as "primus inter pares," first among equals. He or she is the primary ceremonial representative of the community, the "*prime* minister." Since worship is the principal meeting place and unifier for the community, the pastor ought to be the primary worship leader and assume overall responsibility to see that it is well led.

The coadjutant relationship spreads out responsibility, making it humanly possible to bear, yet it produces unclear roles and relationships. To attempt to clarify roles and relationships in accordance with the Biblical model, I would suggest that pastor and deacons form a joint board, perhaps called elders. Patterned after James in the early church, as well as the weak mayor model, the pastor would become voting member of, and would preside over, the board of elders. If this were to happen, one would need to exercise some of the leadership functions of the mayor who presides over the council, clarifying objectives and moving things along tactfully and orderly.

The shared aspect of the pastor's authority involves functioning corporately with lay leadership. To do this in a supportive and cooperative manner, one needs, like the mayor, to attempt to facilitate consensus over any given matter. Sometimes one must be a prophetic voice, calling the congregation to greater faithfulness, though even this is not the pastor's responsibility alone. Most of the time, however, one should present only a general outline, without predetermined conclusions. As presider over the leadership group, this means one must come to know the feelings and perspectives of the lay leadership. One must strive to maintain respect, rapport, and good communication, even in the midst of disagreement. The pastor should encourage co-leaders to initiate proposals, ask them for advice or help, advance their concerns, provide them time to think over new ideas, inform them of the results of ministry, and avoid making some feel left out by too often discussing issues with only select individuals. Furthermore, the wise pastor does not attack others, defend oneself, or call the congregation to side with him or her against the lay leadership, unless it is obvious one is speaking for the majority of the congregation.

Summary

As an authority figure, the church leader represents both God and the church and needs to adopt a unique image or stance. The representative of God is not the ultimate authority. Yet she or he serves to remind people of the One who is. As a representative of the Lord, the church leader must accept the frustrations and high expectations of the people, as well as adopt an image of servanthood. As representative to God one is responsible to publicly and privately intercede in prayer for parishioners. As representative to the local congregation, one symbolizes God and the church in all one says or does. This is especially true in the principal ceremonial function, the leadership of worship, where one symbolizes people's need as well as God's cleansing, blessing, and power. As representative to the wider church one is expected to attend denominational and ecumenical functions, sharing concerns, gaining support, and seeking advice on behalf of both local congregation and the larger body. As representative to the secular community one must encourage support and cooperation between church and community organizations.

The exact nature of the church leader's responsibilities and performance depends on personal charismata, sense of accountability, and the coadjutant nature of relationships with the lay leadership. A church should encourage the development of charismata

within and beyond the local church, provided they do
not jeopardize performance of requisite responsibilities. Moreover, the existence of this charismatic
emphasis implies that experience, self-investment, and
consequent excellence of performance, have an influence on the attainment of authentic authority. The
church leader's sense of accountability to God, as
expressed through accountability to Scripture, individuals within the denominational hierarchy, and especially the congregation, has important consequences
for church leadership and life. Congregational accountability enhances one's ability to accept parishioners' expectations and view one's role as that of a
servant. The coadjutant relationship with lay leadership reveals uniqueness of role, but overlap in function, with the specific nature of one's involvement
depending greatly on abilities. As the *prime* minister, the pastor must guide one's co-leaders in a
process of consensus building. Developing this relationship necessitates much trust and cooperation, and
may require some structural adjustment to stress
plurality of responsibility.

1. Burton Scott Easton, The Pastoral Epistles (New York: Charles Scribner's Sons, 1947), p. 189.

2. Arthur Bromage, Introduction To Municipal Government and Administration, The Century Political Science Series (New York: Appleton-Century-Crofts, Inc., 1950), p. 20.

3. Charles Adrian, Governing Urban America, McGraw-Hill Series in Political Science (2nd ed.; New York: McGraw-Hill Book Company, Inc., 1961), pp. 200-208.

4. League of Wisconsin Municipalities, Handbook for Wisconsin Mayors (Rev. ed.; Madison, Wisconsin: League of Wisconsin Municipalities, 1974), pp. i, 8, and 17.

5. William Anderson and Edward Weidner, American City Government (Rev. ed.; New York: Henry Holt and Company, 1950), pp. 276 and 298.

6. Leonard Ruchelman, ed., Big City Mayors: The Crisis In Urban Politics, taken from introductory material by the editor (Bloomington, Indiana: Indiana University Press, 1969), pp. 4 and 253.

7. Russell Story, The American Municipal Executive, University of Illinois Studies in the Social Sciences, Vol. VII (Urbana, Illinois: University of Illinois under the auspices of the Graduate School, 1918), p. 75.

8. Henry Maier, Challenge To The Cities: An Approach To A Theory of Urban Leadership (New York: Random House, 1966), pp. 4, 10-13.

9. Suzanne Farkas, Urban Lobbying: Mayors In The Federal Arena (New York: New York University Press, 1971), pp. 5-7, 17, and 255.

10. Duane Lockard, "The Mayor As Chief Executive," in Big City Mayors: The Crisis In Urban Politics, ed. by Leonard Ruchelman (Bloomington, Indiana: Indiana University Press, 1969), pp. 142-153.

11. Adrian, p. 268.

12. *Handbook For Wisconsin Mayors*, pp. 3, 9, and 17.

13. John Kotter and Paul Lawrence, *Mayors In Action: Five Approaches To Urban Governance* (New York: John Wiley and Sons, 1974), pp. 105f.

14. Adrian, pp. 177-188 and 243.

15. League of Wisconsin Municipalities, *The Powers and Duties of Mayors In Wisconsin Cities: A Summary of Wisconsin Statutory Requirements* (Madison, Wisconsin: League of Wisconsin Municipalities, 1948), pp. 3-4.

16. Adrian, pp. 172-173.

17. Maier, pp. 130-136 and 179-182.

18. J. Deveroux Weeks, *Handbook For Virginia Mayors and Councilmen* (Richmond, Virginia: Virginia Municipal League and Virginia University Bureau of Public Administration, 1963), p. 12.

19. Elizabeth Smedley, *The Role of the Burgess (Mayor) In Pennsylvania Boroughs* (University Park, Pennsylvania: The Institute of Public Administration, The Pennsylvania State University, 1962), p. 43.

20. Weeks, pp. 37-39.

21. Maier, pp. 183-187.

22. Samuel Southard, *Pastoral Authority In Personal Relationships* (Nashville and New York: Abingdon Press, 1969), pp. 57-58.

23. Hans Kung, *Why Priests?: A Proposal For A New Church Ministry*, trans. by Robert C. Collins (Garden City, New York: Doubleday & Company, Inc., 1972), p. 112.

24. *Ibid.*, pp. 89 and 104.

CHAPTER IX

THE FINAL PICTURE

The final picture or conception of leadership role and authority in the church must include material drawn from both the Biblical and historical principles and the secular models. We must embrace all these images at once, discovering a general perspective common to them all. The process is much like Paul Minear's "synoptic thinking" approach to interrelating the Biblical images of the early church.[1] The result will be a vision of the ideal conception of leadership role and authority for today. Finding common threads throughout the Biblical and secular models should strongly indicate the direction in which both pastoral and lay callings are headed.

First, I will review the Biblical norms for leadership role and authority in light of the predominant contemporary need for a sense of community. The four Biblical functions (eldership, overseeing, teaching, and shepherding) all contribute to the contemporary understanding of authority, administration, teaching, and care, respectively. Of these, administration must become predominant. It is the one around which, and toward which, everything else builds. For it is the one function most critical in developing the ministry of the laity which, in turn, is necessary for building community. The purpose of authority then becomes the personification of the communal traditions and authority which undergird the very life of the body of Christ. The purpose of care is to sustain, guide, reconcile, and heal lonely, isolated people who are striving to minister effectively according to their gifts. The purpose of teaching becomes the equipping of the laity, with both character and skills, for the work of ministry and the building up of the body of Christ. Regarding authority, any contemporary conception must maintain the Biblical balance of the charismatic and official bases of authority, plus its partly shared, partly unique nature. Furthermore, we need to retain the three traditional sources of authority (communal, scriptural, and individual), giving predominance to the first. In this light, interpretation of the Scriptures should focus on communal rather than individual interpretations. In addition, we need to see individuals, when functioning as authority figures, primarily as representatives of the community.

To gain insight into the various functions, I have previously explored four secular models, parallel to each of the leadership functions. In putting the pieces together, there are certain characteristics we discover that are central to the contemporary expression of each function. First, each one attempts to build a sense of community. Second, each emphasizes positive development, or growth, of both individuals and the whole church, rather than a negative approach of correcting problems or misconceptions. Third, each function requires close ties, on the part of leadership, to the personal experience of parishioners. Fourth, each function stresses the need to adapt one's understanding of leadership to the particular setting, including sensitivity to the needs and abilities of both individuals and the local church. Consequently, the following should characterize the contemporary conception of leadership role and authority in the church. It should be community building, growth oriented, experience related, and individually adapted. The first three sections provide a synopsis of the ideal conception for which we must aim; the last addresses the need to arrive at an operating conception for specific churches and church leaders.

Community Building

As we have seen from the above analysis of contemporary needs, the focus of church leadership role and authority is on the development of the church as a community. The four leadership functions, as derived from the various secular models, all bear this out. Administration entails the development of team ministries, encouragement of the exercise of personal gifts on behalf of the whole congregation, and the provision of direction for the whole church. Teaching includes the development of ministry skills in relation to others within the congregation and often takes place within a close-knit, small group setting. Care involves the corporate exercise of church discipline, and the promotion of mutual shepherding, especially diagnostic and preventive, by lay members. Authority derives primarily from one's accountability to the community, and is a shared authority between pastor and lay leadership. In all these functions, one works, not so much with the individual, as with the church body, in the context of a covenant of shared responsibility. One strives to bring into being a people of God who will faithfully fulfill the mission of the church and the will of God. To do this one must function as a "playing coach," willing to step into the fray oneself, yet not removing responsibility from the people. One's primary task is to see that things get done, more than to do them oneself.

The emphasis on community building has implications for the structure of church government and the programming of church activities, as well as the place of the church leader in relation to both. Each of the models for the four functions involves the pastor working with a group of lay persons, who, in turn, minister in a similar way to the other laity and those beyond the church. Particularly, as we consider the shared nature of authority, it makes most sense if this group, with whom the pastor relates most closely, is composed of the deacons or lay leadership. I would propose that, together, pastor and deacons form a board of elders. Within this board the pastor would become an authority figure for the others, presiding over meetings. Furthermore, one would care for them in all their needs, teach them regarding the faith and the ministry, and supervise their involvement in mission, in order that they may do all these things for the rest of the church. It may help to limit each person's responsibilities by dividing them among the members of the board, as the model for administration recommends. In this way, each deacon would take responsibility for the oversight of certain areas of the church's ministry, for the care of certain individuals, or for the quality of life of certain church groups. We can also see the influence of the community building emphasis in the structure of the governing board, as already observed within the models for administration and authority. In order to promote the greatest sense of joint mission and broad participation, the church would do well to structure the governing board so as to include the board of elders, representatives of various church groups, and representatives at large. Such a structure should serve to focus the governing board's attention on the ministry of its small groups.

The community building emphasis also focuses attention on interpersonal relationships within the church. All four secular models stress open dialogue communication and the need for cooperation by all. Consequently, consensus building and reconciliation, interpersonal and divine-human, are goals for all aspects of leadership functioning. The church leader must serve as negotiator and intercessor among, and on behalf of, the people. One is the servant, serving their persons, their understandings, and their ministries. This requires an understanding of both the

167

general dynamics of human relationships, and the specific character of the class of people with whom one is working, as documented in each of the models.

Growth Oriented

Each of the four models suggests that leadership role and authority ought to be so conceived as to promote growth into Christian maturity on the part of both lay people and pastor. The good administrator stresses the positive in the evaluation process of the ministry of church and individuals. The church leader as authority figure undergirds a person, giving one a firm foundation from which growth can take place. In care and teaching the whole purpose is to promote growth. This positive orientation is much more constructive than that of problemsolving or troubleshooting. It is not crisis intervention, but continual stimulation, that best characterizes contemporary ministry.

All the models portray the church leader as a trainer or enabler, empowering others to mature and develop as persons, and assisting them to choose ministries which fit their capabilities. One sustains, guides, and heals, not only as caring person, ministering to individuals' emotional needs, but also as administrator, teacher, and authority figure. As administrator one guides both individuals and church, sustains the capabilities of the former, and heals working relationships within the latter. As a teacher one also guides both individuals and the church, and sustains and heals their minds. As an authority figure one sustains, guides, and heals through the use of one's image and character. In all this, one both acts personally as a resource person, and draws upon outside resources, such as educators and caring persons.

The whole point of the church leader's efforts is to cultivate self-direction on the part of individuals. In each model there is concern that every person establish one's own objectives and patterns for growth. Two models, administration and care (under the section "guiding"), urge the church leader to help people identify purposes, analyze situations, form goals, devise alternative strategies, choose a procedure, and set out the necessary steps. Afterward, one must help them to evaluate themselves, assessing areas of growth and points needing growth. In this process the church leader can personally stimulate them to search for new insights, point to resources, and summarize learnings. But one cannot control the rate or direction of growth. One is a catalyst and integrator for the growth pains and labors of both individuals and the congregation. As authority figure, caring person, teacher, and administrator, one can pull together their experiences, emotions, learnings, and tasks, respectively. In order to assist this growth, the church leader must also be a growing person, setting one's own goals, determining and developing one's own personal charismata, as well as ascertaining one's limitations, learning from, and utilizing, one's own experience. One's style should be that of openness to evaluation and change, that one might model for others what it means to grow in service to Christ.

Experience Related

It is appropriate that ecclesiastical leadership role and authority be related to experience, since the gospel which we all serve is rooted in life experiences. This means that everything the church leader does should touch the practical side of life. Administration, teaching and preaching, care of persons, and the expressions of authority, should all begin and end at points where people are living their lives. In exercising each function, the church leader must help the parishioner tie the new input to past and present experiences. To do this, one must, as much as possible, adapt one's ministry to the needs of individuals, and help them to reflect on their experiences. One must enter their frames of reference to discover the task which fits each one's capabilities and the expectations which govern their demands upon the pastor or lay leader. One must keep this in mind when one provides new information or perspectives in teaching, in supervision of individuals' ministries, or in ministries of guidance and reconciliation. One must accept their resistances to learning, to performing a particular task, to counseling, or to accepting the leader's fallibility.

In addition, even the church leader-parishioner encounter should become an experience which the parishioner will fondly remember. The most indelible and fruitful experiences are those which carry a dramatic quality, those which help create a leadership image in the mind of the parishioner. Worship and preaching especially afford such an opportunity, yet other functions can serve the same purpose. They all provide events in which one reminds people of God. As an authority figure, the experiencing of one's very presence, one's person, acts as a reminder of God, equally as much as the experiencing of one's teaching, preaching, or administration. Expressions of care, concern, and emotional support, as demonstrated through any of the functions, are important parts of the parishioner's experience of the leader, and ultimately, of God. In order to provide such an experience, the church leader must be an open person. As a teacher one must be capable of being taught. As an administrator one needs to consult one's parishioners. As a caring person one needs to listen to their story. As an authority figure one needs to ascertain and understand their concerns. One must embody the same openness which one would hope to develop in them. Moreover, one has to invest oneself in the caring, the administration, the preaching and teaching, and the exercise of authority. Only through such demonstration and participation can the parishioners experience an encounter which is at all dramatic.

Individually Adapted

Each church is different, and conceives of leadership role and authority in a slightly different way. The fact that we are presently in a state of flux between the passing of one predominant function and the emergence of another, adds to the variety of operational conceptions of leadership role and authority present in our churches. In addition, each leader is a unique person, gifted with one's own identity, one's own set of personal charismata (capabilities, interests, and style), one's own experiences, one's own degree of confidence, and one's own understanding of servanthood. Lay people also possess a variety of gifts. Those which they have, or lack, determine, to some degree, what tasks the leader must perform. Consequently, we need to adapt the ideal conception to the specific leader and church, fitting both leadership role and authority to the unique relationship. Whenever a new pastor comes to a church, a new role and new understanding of authority must come into being. The vision and needs within the congregation must interact with those the pastor brings, resulting in a new working relationship.

Many churches are still very much entrenched in conceptions of leadership role and authority which are not centered around the predominance of administration or of communal authority. For this reason, and because it is easier for one person, than for a group, to shift positions, the leader sometimes needs to give most of one's attention to another function or source of authority which is more traditionally acceptable. To once again draw a parallel with Maslow's "hierarchy of needs," there are exceptions to the normal tendency to fulfill the most basic needs of food or safety before meeting the more complex ones. Those who sacrifice for ethical, social, or religious values are good examples.[2] In the same way teaching or preaching, pastoral care or authority may become predominant for a particular church and pastor. Likewise, Scripture or certain individuals may become predominant sources of authority in a particular location. However, in this case it is not out of desire, but out of necessity, that the exception is made. Church and leadership must not lose sight of the end toward which they are building, even if the needs of the church demand focusing on another function or source of authority.

Any changes toward the preferred conception of leadership role and authority should be gradual. The church leader should take care to not move the security rocks from under a person or a church. If people are accustomed to looking to either Scripture or the Bishop as the final authority, it will do little good to insist that they immediately change their perspective. Including them in the decision-making accomplishes the desired result without making an issue out of it. If someone, or some group, perceives care as most basic, then the leader should not suddenly decrease the amount of visitation to those persons. If a particular church views preaching as central, than the leader had better not cut the time spent on sermon in favor of administrative or supervisory responsibilities. If a particular lay leader is not trained, or capable of functioning, in a particular leadership capacity, then the pastor needs to accept him or her with the abilities he or she has, even if it means being unable to delegate a responsibility in which the pastor is not particularly gifted. In addition, one should give recognition to the ways in which the lay leader already grasps the significance of certain aspects of his or her calling. In short, the church leader must accept both the expectations and the limitations of the people, giving them positive perspectives on the pastor and lay leaders, on themselves, and on their joint ministry.

The church leader must work together with the people to increase the growth and awareness of all, regarding the conception of leadership role and authority most needed at present, and that toward which they are developing. At points of conflict one must be careful not to react, but to negotiate with them in a spirit of openness, and to motivate them to fulfill more of their potential. Such a process requires a strong sense of direction on the part of all parties. Both leader and congregation need to develop clear positions in order to have somewhere from which to negotiate. However, after doing this preliminary task, they must be able to listen to one another and work together, reviewing and modifying each other's proposals. When they do agree it is important to, once again, check the proposed operating conception against the stated mission of the church and communicate the nature of the agreement to the entire congregation. Finally, they will periodically need to review and update this covenant of shared responsibility in order to continually progress toward the desired predominance of administrative function and communal authority.

NOTES

1. Paul S. Minear, _Images of the Church In The New Testament_ (Philadelphia: The Westminster Press, 1960), p. 221.

2. Abraham H. Maslow, _Motivation and Personality_ (2nd ed.; New York: Harper and Row, 1970), p. 99.

BIBLIOGRAPHY

BOOKS

Adams, Arthur. *Pastoral Administration*. Philadelphia:
Westminster Press, 1964.

Adrian, Charles. *Governing Urban America*. McGraw-
Hill Series In Political Science. 2nd ed.
New York: McGraw-Hill Book Company, Inc.,
1961.

Anderson, William, and Weidner, Edward. *American City
Government*. Rev. ed. New York: Henry Holt &
Co., 1950.

Babin, David E. *Week In - Week Out: A New Look At
Liturgical Preaching*. New York: The Seabury Press, 1976.

Bauer, Walter. *A Greek-English Lexicon of the New
Testament and Other Early Christian Liter-
ature*. Translated and adapted by William F.
Arndt and F. Wilbur Gringrich. Chicago:
University of Chicago Press, 1957.

Blake, Robert R. and Mouton, Jane Srygley. *Building A
Dynamic Corporation Through Grid Organization Development*. Addison-Wesley Series on
Organization Development. Reading, Massachusetts: Addison-Wesley Publishing Co., 1969.

_____, and _____. *Corporate Excellence
Through Grid Organizational Development*.
Houston, Texas: Scientific Methods, Inc.,
1975.

_____, and _____. *The Grid for Super-
visory Effectiveness*. Austin, Texas:
Scientific Methods, Inc., 1975.

_____, and _____. *The Managerial Grid:
Key Orientations For Achieving Productivity
Through People*. Houston, Texas: Gulf
Publishing Co., 1964.

Bromage, Arthur. <u>Introduction To Municipal Government Administration</u>. The Century Political Science Series. New York: Appleton-Century-Crofts, Inc., 1950.

Brow, Robert. <u>Religion and Ideas</u>. Chicago: Inter-Varsity Press, 1966.

Brown, Raymond E. <u>The Gospel According To John (XIII-XXI)</u>. Vol. 29:2 of <u>The Anchor Bible</u>. Edited by William F. Albright and David N. Freedman. Garden City, New York: Doubleday and Co., Inc., 1970.

Button, Leslie. <u>Discovery and Experience</u>. London: Oxford University Press, 1971.

Campenhausen, Hans von. <u>Ecclesiastical Authority and Spiritual Power In The Church of the First Three Centuries</u>. Translated by J. A. Baker. Stanford, California: Stanford University Press, 1969.

Clebsch, William A. and Jaekle, Charles R. <u>Pastoral Care In Historical Perspective</u>. Englewood Cliffs, New Jersey: Prentice-Hall, Inc., 1964.

Deanesly, Margaret. <u>A History of the Medieval Church 590-1500</u>. 8th ed. London: Unwin Brothers Limited, 1954.

Dibelius, Martin and Conzelmann, Hans. <u>The Pastoral Epistles: A Commentary On The Pastoral Epistles</u>. Edited by Helmut Koester. Translated by Philip Buttolph and Adela Yarbro. Philadelphia: Fortress Press, 1972.

Drucker, Peter F. <u>Management: Task, Responsibilities, Practices</u>. New York: Harper and Row, Publishers, 1973.

_____. <u>The Practice of Management</u>. New York: Harper, 1954.

Easton, Burton Scott. <u>The Pastoral Epistles</u>. New York: Charles Scribner's Sons, 1947.

Farkas, Suzanne. <u>Urban Lobbying: Mayors In The Federal Arena</u>. New York: New York University Press, 1971.

Ferguson, Wallace K. A Survey of European Civiliza-
    tion Part One to 1660. Edited by William L.
    Langer. 3rd. ed. Boston: Houghton Mifflin
    Co., 1962.

Glasse, James D. Profession: Minister. Nashville and
    New York: Abingdon Press, 1968.

Holmes, Urban T. III. The Future Shape of Ministry: A
    Theological Projection. New York: The
    Seabury Press, 1971.

Hunter, George. Theological Field Education. Newton
    Centre, Massachusetts: The Boston Theolog-
    ical Institute, 1977.

Jud, Gerald J.; Mills, Edgar W.; and Burch, Genevieve
    Walters. Ex-pastors: Why Men Leave The
    Parish Ministry. Philadelphia: United
    Church Press, 1970.

Kaesemann, Ernst. Essays On New Testament Themes.
    Translated by W. J. Montague. Naperville,
    Illinois: Alec R. Allenson, Inc., 1964.

Kaufmann, Yehezkel. The Religion of Israel. Trans-
    lated and abridged by Moshe Greenberg.
    Chicago: University of Chicago Press, 1960.

Klink, Thomas. Depth Perspectives In Pastoral Work.
    Successful Pastoral Counseling Series.
    Philadelphia: Fortress Press, 1969.

Kotter, John and Lawrence, Paul. Mayors in Action:
    Five Approaches to Urban Governance. New
    York: John Wiley and Sons, 1974.

Kung, Hans. The Church. Translated by Ray and
    Rosaleen Ockenden, New York: Sheed and
    Ward, 1967.

_____. Why Priests? A Proposal For A New Church
    Ministry. Translated by Robert C. Collins.
    Garden City, New York: Doubleday & Company,
    Inc., 1972.

Leech, Kenneth. Soul Friend: The Practice of
    Christian Sprituality. San Francisco:
    Harper and Row, Publishers, 1977.

177

Maier, Henry. <u>Challenge To The Cities: An Approach To A Theory of Urban Leadership</u>. New York: Random House, 1966.

Maslow, Abraham H. <u>Motivation and Personality</u>. 2nd. ed. New York: Harper and Row, 1970.

McNeill, John T. <u>A History of The Cure of Souls</u>. New York: Harper and Brother Publishers, 1951.

Minear, Paul S. <u>Images of the Church in the New Testament</u>. Philadelphia: The Westminster Press, 1960.

Niebuhr, H. Richard. <u>The Purpose of the Church and Its Ministry: Reflections on the Aims of Theological Education</u>. New York: Harper and Brothers, 1956.

Palmer, R. R. <u>A History of the Modern World</u>. Revised with the collaboration of Joel Colton. 2nd ed. New York: Alfred A. Knopf, Inc., 1956.

Purkiser, W. T. <u>The New Testament Image of the Ministry</u>. Kansas City, Missouri: Beacon Hill Press of Kansas City, 1969.

Ruchelman, Leonard, ed. <u>Big City Mayors: The Crisis In Urban Politics</u>. Bloomington, Indiana: Indiana University Press, 1969.

Schweizer, Eduard. <u>Church Order in The New Testament</u>. Translated by Frank Clarke. Naperville, Illinois: Alec R. Allenson, Inc., 1961.

Southard, Samuel. <u>Pastoral Authority in Personal Relationships</u>. Nashville and New York: Abingdon Press, 1969.

Story, Russell. <u>The American Municipal Executive</u>. University of Illinois Studies in the Social Sciences. Vol. VII. Urbana, Illinois: University of Illinois under the auspices of the Graduate School, 1918.

Streeter, Burnett H. <u>The Primitive Church</u>. London: MacMillan and Co., 1929.

Trueblood, D. Elton. <u>The Company of the Committed</u>. New York: Harper and Row, 1961.

Walker, Williston. A History of the Christian Church. Revised by Cyril Richardson, Wilhelm Pauck, and Robert Handy. New York: Charles Scribner's Sons, 1959.

Wand, J. W. C. A History of the Early Church To A.D. 500. 4th ed. Norwich, Great Britain: Jarrold and Sons Ltd., 1963.

ARTICLES

Andrus, Len Hughes and Geyman, John P. "Managing the Health Care Team." Family Practice. Edited by Howard Conn, Robert Rakel, and Thomas Johnson. Philadelphia: W.B. Saunders Co., 1973.

Beyer, Hermann W. "ἐπισκέπτομαι, ἐπισκοπέω, ἐπισκοπή, ἐπίσκοπος, ἀλλοτπιεπίσκοπος." Theological Dictionary of the New Testament. Vol. II. Edited by Gerhard Kittel. Translated by Geoffrey W. Bromiley. Grand Rapids: William B. Eerdmans Pub. Co., 1964.

Blake, Robert R.; Mouton, Jane S.; Barnes, Louis B.; and Greiner, Larry E. "Breakthrough In Organizational Development." Harvard Business Review (November-December, 1964), 133-155.

Bornkamm, Gunther. "πρέσβυς, πρεσβύτερος, πρεσβύτης, συμπρεσβύτερος, πρεσβυτέριον, πρεσβέυω." Theological Dictionary of the New Testament. Vol. VI. Edited by Gerhard Kittel. Translated by Geoffrey W. Bromiley. Grand Rapids: William B. Eerdmans Pub. Co., 1968.

Bruner, Jerome. "After John Dewey, What?" American Education Today. Edited by Paul Woodring and John Scanlon. 4th ed. New York: McGraw-Hill Book Company, Inc., 1963.

Curry, Hiram and Grant, Silas. "Role of the Family Physician." Family Practice. Edited by Howard Conn, Robert Rakel, and Thomas Johnson. Philadelphia: W.B. Saunders Co., 1973.

Eastman, Francis. "The Open Church School." A Colloquy on Christian Education. Edited by John Westerhoff III. Philadelphia: United Church Press, 1972.

Friedrich, Gerhard. "εὐαγγελίζομαι, εὐαγγέλιον, προευαγγελίζομαι, εὐαγγελιστής." Theological Dictionary of the New Testament. Vol. II. Edited by Gerhard Kittel. Translated by Geoffrey W. Bromiley. Grand Rapids: William B. Eerdmans Pub. Co., 1964.

Froelich, Robert and Verby, Jack. "Interviewing Techniques." Family Practice. Edited by Howard Conn, Robert Rakel, and Thomas Johnson. Philadelphia: W.B. Saunders Co., 1973.

Jeremias, Joachim. "ποιμήν, ἀρχιποίμην, ποιμαίνω, ποίμνη, ποίμνιον." Theological Dictionary of the New Testament. Vol. VI. Edited by Gerhard Kittel. Translated by Geoffrey W. Bromiley. Grand Rapids: William B. Eerdmans Pub. Co., 1968.

Johnson, Mauritz. "The Rise and Fall of 'Life Adjustment.'" American Education Today. Edited by Paul Woodring and John Scanlon. 4th ed. New York: McGraw-Hill Book Company, Inc., 1963.

Klink, Thomas W. "Supervision As A Routine Process In Professional Education for Ministry." Typewritten paper reprnted in the Duke Divinity School Review, 1968.

Lockard, Duane. "The Mayor As Chief Executive." Big City Mayors: The Crisis In Urban Politics. Edited by Leonard Ruchelman. Bloomington, Indiana: Indiana University Press, 1969.

Mitzel, Harold. "The Impending Instruction Revolution." Individualized Instruction And Learning. Compiled and edited by Madan Mohan and Ronald Hull. Chicago: Nelson Hall Co., 1974.

Pace, J. Blair. "Rehabilitation." Family Practice. Edited by Howard Conn, Robert Rakel, and Thomas Johnson. Philadelphia: W.B. Saunders Co., 1973.

Peske, Derek; Tanner, Libby; and Aschenbrener, Thomas. "The Allied Health Professions." Family Practice. Edited by Howard Conn, Robert Rakel, and Thomas Johnson. Philadelphia: W.B. Saunders Co., 1973.

Phillips, Theodore. "The Preventive Attitude." Family Practice. Edited by Howard Conn, Robert Rakel, and Thomas Johnson. Philadelphia: W.B. Saunders Co., 1973.

Rengstorf, Karl H. "ἀποστέλλω, ἐξαποστέλλω, ἀπόστολος, ψευδαπόστολος, ἀποστολή." Theological Dictionary of the New Testament. Vol. I. Edited by Gerhard Kittel. Translated by Geoffrey W. Bromiley. Grand Rapids: William B. Eerdmans Pub. Co., 1964.

_____. "διδάσκω, διδάσκαλος, νομοδιδάσκαλος, καλοδιδάσκαλος, ψευδοδιδάσκαλος, διδασκαλία, ἑτεροδιδασκαλέω, διδαχή, διδακτός, διδακτικός." Theological Dictionary of the New Testament. Vol. II. Edited by Gerhard Kittel. Translated by Geoffrey W. Bromiley. Grand Rapids: William B. Eerdmans Pub. Co., 1964.

Roek, Robert and Baisden, C. Robert. "Health Screening: Early Detection of Disease." Family Practice. Edited by Howard Conn, Robert Rakel, and Thomas Johnson. Philadelphia: W.B. Saunders Co., 1973.

Stokes, Joseph III and Schneiderman, L. J. "The Clinical Practice of Preventive Medicine." Family Practice. Edited by Howard Conn, Robert Rakel, and Thomas Johnson. Philadelphia: W.B. Saunders Co., 1973.

Williams, Tennyson and Corely, J.B. "The Management of Chronic Illness." Family Practice. Edited by Howard Conn, Robert Rakel, and Thomas Johnson. Philadelphia: W.B. Saunders Co., 1973.

HANDBOOKS, MANUALS, REPORTS, OUTLINES, TAPES

Advisory manual prepared by the Committee on Medical
Economics of the American Academy of General
Practice. Raymond Kahn, Chairman. Organi-
zation and Management of Family Practice.
Kansas City, Missouri: American Academy of
General Practice, 1968.

American R. D. M. Corporation. A Study Outline For
World History. New York: American R. D. M.
Corporation, 1962.

Johnson, Ben. Foundations for the Emerging Church:
Contemporary Expression, Session 4 of tape.
Waco, Texas: Word Publications, 1971.

League of Wisconsin Municipalities. Handbook for Wisconsin Mayors. Rev. ed. Madison, Wisconsin:
League of Wisconsin Municipalities, 1974.

_____. The Powers and Duties of Mayors in
Wisconsin Cities: A Summary of Wisconsin
Statutory Requirements. Madison, Wisconsin:
League of Wisconsin Municipalities, 1948.

Report of the Ad Hoc Committee on Education for Family
Practice of the Council on Medical Educa-
tion, American Medical Association. William
Willard, Chairman. Meeting The Challenge of
Family Practice. Chicago: Council on
Medical Education, American Medical Associa-
tion, 1966.

Smedley, Elizabeth. The Role of the Burgess (Mayor)
In Pennsylvania Boroughs. University Park,
Pennsylvania: The Institute of Public
Administration, The Pennsylvania State
University, 1962.

Weeks, J. Deveroux. Handbook For Virginia Mayors and
Councilmen. Richmond, Virginia: Virginia
Municipal League and Virginia University
Bureau of Public Administration, 1963.

INDEX

A

Accountability 88, 99, 148-50,
155-60, 166
Accountable 148, 151, 155, 157
Administer(ed)(ring) 16, 19,
124, 137
Administration 6, 11, 13, 47,
54, 56, 76, 83, 88-91, 141,
151, 165-71
Administrative 63, 88-91, 96-
102, 130, 149, 171-72
Administrator(s) 10, 83, 89-
91, 96, 101, 102, 145, 168-70
Apostle(ship) 5-15, 19, 46
Apostolic 10, 44-8, 76, 77

B

Bible v, 55, 59-62, 111-17,
137
Biblical xiv, xvi, 23, 35, 37,
80, 88, 113-15, 127, 132,
134, 137, 145, 156-59, 165
Biblicism 60
Bishop(s) 9-16, 44-58, 154,
158

C

Care(s) 24-6, 30-3, 47, 50-
55, 74-8, 123-41, 165-71
Careful(ly) 129, 136, 172
Caretaker 127, 129, 134-37,
141, 148
Communal 150, 158, 165, 171,
172
Communica(te)(tion) 158, 159,
167, 172
Communion 132-36, 159

Community 4-18, 63, 73-8, 80,
83, 87, 96, 108, 110, 118,
123, 127, 130, 135, 137,
145-60, 165-67
Confess 50, 135
Confession(s)(al) 50-53, 135,
141
Confessor(s) 48, 57, 135
Coordination 147
Counseling 126-29, 133-36,
139, 141
Counselor(s) 13, 139

D

Deacon(s) 6, 9-11, 16, 19, 32,
137-40, 159, 167
Disciple(ship) 25, 34, 38,
45, 116, 139
Discipline(s)(ing) 29-33, 46-
50, 53, 61, 62, 109, 135,
136, 141, 166,
Discipling 37, 38

E

Ecumenical 154, 160
Elder(s) 4-9, 12-9, 27-35,
75, 78, 79, 137, 145, 159,
167
Eldership 15, 19, 23, 27, 44,
45, 49-56, 78, 79, 145, 165
Empowering 139, 168
Enable(r)(s)(ing) 26, 38, 39,
90, 97, 107, 110, 134, 168
Equip(pers)(ping) 23, 33, 38,
78, 165
Eucharist(ic) 44, 45, 51, 56,
62, 158
Evangelism 155
Evangelist(s) 4, 6, 12, 19,
33, 34, 118, 156, 157

183

185

ABOUT THE AUTHOR

David Steele has been an ordained minister in the United Church of Christ for 15 years and has a Doctor of Ministry in pastoral care from Andover Newton Theological School. Dr. Steele was pastor of Pilgrim Congregational Church in Cambridge, Massachusetts for 14 years. For six years he was also an instructor, and adjunct faculty, in field education supervisory training at Gordon-Cromwell Theological Seminary. After a year's sabbatical at Church of the Savior, and internship at Institute for Policy Studies, both in Washington, D.C., Dr. Steele has been interim pastoring in the Washington area and has worked at Search for Common Ground, a public policy institute which deals with common security issues in East-West relations.

Currently Dr. Steele is a post-graduate student at New College, University of Edinburgh, Scotland, studying for a Ph.D. in spirituality and politics.